Advent and Psychic Birth

✝

Mariann Burke

PAULIST PRESS
New York and Mahwah, N.J.

242.33
Bu A

Library of Congress Cataloging-in-Publication Data

Burke, Mariann.
    Advent and psychic birth / Mariann Burke.
        p.   cm.
    Includes bibliographical references.
    ISBN 0-8091-3431-4 (pbk.)
    1. Advent. 2. Self-actualization (Psychology)—Religious aspects—Christianity.   3. Femininity (Philosophy)   4. Femininity of God.
5. Mary, Blessed Virgin, Saint—Symbolism.   6. Jesus Christ—Mythological interpretations.   I. Title.
BV40.B77   1993
242'.33—dc20   93-19318
                                                                      CIP

Published by Paulist Press
997 Macarthur Boulevard
Mahwah, New Jersey 07430

Printed and bound in the
United States of America

Contents

FOR ROGER RADLOFF *in memoriam,*

MARY BRINER AND PAUL BRUTSCHE

Acknowledgments

I want to express my gratitude to my brother Daniel who in innumerable ways showed his care and enthusiastic support over the years from the time the idea for this book first took shape, my brother Ed for helping me to "hang loose," Ann B. Ulanov, Robert Baer CSP, John Hill and Fred Gustafson, for reading the manuscript and offering valuable suggestions, Kathleen Hughes, RSCJ for suggesting helpful resources, Maryellen Harmon, RSCJ for her keen insights and warm friendship, Walter Wink who many years ago at Union Theological Seminary opened new pathways for personalizing the biblical message and who first introduced me to the writings of C.G. Jung. And I want to thank my analysands for continuing to teach me about the mysterious ways of the psyche.

Everything psychic is pregnant with the future.
—C.G. Jung

Introduction

Meister Eckhart in a Christmas sermon paraphrasing St. Augustine says of Christ's birth, "This birth is always happening. And yet, if it does not occur in me, how could it help me? Everything depends on that."[1] The thesis of this book is that our own psychological "birth" is related to the "birth" of God within us, and that this birth is "always happening." The paradox is that we long for this birth and yet we fear it. For centuries our unconscious fears and longing have been mirrored and "contained" in the religious dogma and symbolism of the church, a channel to the riverbed of the unconscious. But in a church and a culture that generally devalues the feminine realm—earth, the body, sexuality, instinct—these energies flow back into the psyche. Today the longing for consciousness and the integration of these energies have led many to leave the church which, they feel, no longer speaks to their needs. Others find spiritual fulfillment in a strong adherence to traditional doctrinal and Biblical interpretation. Still others, in increasing numbers, find that a more personal inner journey leads not only to greater self-awareness, but also to a richer appreciation of their religious heritage.

My approach throughout these pages is to try to make connections between the archetypal images and personal experience, in both ancient and modern modalities, through associations, amplifications and clinical material. In one sense this approach has evolved out of my training in analytical psychology. Yet it has become deeply personal and flows out of my own felt sense of the Advent imagery and my own journey toward psychic birth. Far from diminishing my faith in Christ, it has broadened and deepened my understanding of the meaning of incarnation. Jung writes: "The efficacy of dogma by no means rests on Christ's unique historical reality but on its own symbolic nature, by virtue of which it expresses a more or less ubiquitous psychological assumption quite independent of the existence of any dogma."[2] On first reading these words we may feel that Jung is undermining dogma and Christ's mission on earth, yet our own experience as it relates to the underlying pattern of dogma, can only serve to enrich its meaning. "In religious matters . . . we cannot understand a thing until we have experienced it inwardly . . . for it is in this experience that the connection between the psyche and the outward image or creed is revealed. . . ."[3]

For each of us the image that speaks to us differs. For some it is an image from the Bible or from another religious tradition, while for others it is a dream image, or an image that seems to surface directly from the body. Each of these can be received as "messages" from God.

If we look at the biblical poetry of Advent in a more personal way, we find that while it belongs to the Hebrew and Christian scriptures, it transcends both. Beginning in darkness and destruction and ending in light and rebirth, Advent imagery represents a mythic or archetypal pattern. The Advent call to awaken from sleep is a call to follow the way of consciousness, to search for the inestimable gift, the treasure of the "hidden" self as well as the *Imago Dei* which carries the power to revitalize us both as individuals and communities. Symbolically, the four Sundays of Advent remind us of the quarternity and of wholeness, as does the familiar Advent wreath with its four candles, one lighted each week suggesting the gradual dissipation of inner and outer darkness. During the first three weeks of the Advent liturgy, the tone is decidedly one of action and movement, beginning with the Baptist's call to prepare a way. With the desert "transition" the tone changes, and during the fourth week the Virgin appears, strong, questioning, willing to trust in the unknown. As in any religious initiation we are led to participate in a new dimension of life. Here, if we can contact our own "virgin energies," we listen as the angel speaks and we, in silence, like Mary, wait as the earth "buds forth a savior."

In chapter 1 we shall look at the background of the Advent season in the myths and practices underlying the winter solstice festivals, when our ancestors anticipated the return of the sun which had "disappeared." We shall look in particular at the myth of eternal return, in which the end of the year is celebrated analogously as a death, a return to chaos, and a renewal of time, of society and of each person. Our ancestors' sense of expectancy mirrors our own as we look at material from the oldest celebration of New Year in ancient Babylonia, noting, too, an earlier time, when the "birth of the new child or sun" came, not following the death of the old king and the restoration of the new, but out of the all-encompassing Earth Mother. The myth of eternal return is patterned after the creation myth in which life comes out of the "void," at the word of God. From a psychological perspective the myth reflects our own anticipation of new life even in the midst of our experience of "chaos" and darkness.

Longing is the theme of chapter 2, our own longing for rebirth and wholeness. We shall look at the ancient practice of the alchemists and at their *opus* in which they projected into matter their own psychic aspirations and their longing for God and for self. As Advent celebrates the feminine mystery of birth, so the alchemists intuited rebirth from the earth and from matter. Though they understood little about matter, they worked in their laboratory watching the effect of fire on the particles of earth they had placed in the round vessel, or *vas*. Through meditation and work they sought a more personal experience of incarnation. Through "operations" they performed on matter, the operations of water (*solutio*), air (*sublimatio*), fire (*calcinatio*), and earth (*coagulatio*), they "brought forth" their "stone" or "Child," names they gave to the goal of their work, the inner "gold" of immortality. We will make some connections between the color worlds of the alchemists, the *nigredo* (black), *albedo* (white), and *rubedo* (red), and the stages represented in the Advent biblical imagery.

Hope is the theme in chapter 3, hope imaged by the savior child-god, the One who restores and frees us. The child-god represents one aspect of our own psyche together with the "dream" child, the real child, the divine child. Men and women in therapy often dream of children and infants, perhaps representing possibilities to be developed psychically. We shall look at two clinical vignettes in which women express their desire to have a baby. In some cases such an image may represent hope hidden under a sense of isolation and depression. Hope in its religious expression reaches a pitch of intensity during Advent with the "O" Antiphons. We shall look at these prayers as expressions of our longing for Christ as well as for our own hope for release from loneliness and fear.

Chapter 4 leads us back to beginnings where we encounter our fear. We are called to awaken and awakening to fuller consciousness can be painful and frightening. Key images here are the mountain, in mythology regarded as the Center of the World, the place of renewal and rebirth. Biblical passages recounting destruction by water and fire are also read during the first week of the Advent liturgy reminding us of the "return to chaos" in the solstice festivals, a prerequisite to "awakening" the sun. Psychologically this awakening can be viewed as a call to further development or, as in the case of movement toward "psychic birth," to a separation of the ego from the paradisical oneness of containment. Psychologically, this painful separation both from the mother and from the unconscious is needed for further development of the ego and a more secure sense of self.

In the wilderness our fear gives way to sadness and our sadness to anger. We need our anger, for it helps us to find our way. The wilderness journey is by far the longest stage in the way to rebirth. Jung tells us that there is no clear way; the way is made up of fateful detours and wrong turnings. The Baptist calls us to minister to the poor, psychologically to recognize and embrace the "poor" in ourselves. The parts we fear and hate, perhaps our anger and rage, our inner fierce "animals" need to be wrestled with in the wilderness of our psyche. Often the "demons" release their energies as light and power for movement into birth. In the wilderness we experience both demonic fire and life-giving waters, as we move into a period of "waiting" for the dawn.

After a night of darkness, we begin to experience the joy hidden within our own darkness. The dew symbolizes the awakening of joy. In chapter 6 we look at Mary as the Virgin and Mother, psychologically speaking the feminine side of God. While the motifs of fire and water are dominant during the wilderness sojourn, now we focus on air and earth motifs. The "child" of the alchemists comes out of the earth, that is, the human personality, and is nourished by all the elements. So we, too, in our journey to "birth" need to sense our spiritual "center" as giving purpose and meaning for our life. Yet while we look to heaven, or to "ideal" people in our lives to search for this center, we must come down to earth, to "embody" and to feel our body as "home" and cradle for our new life, the "child of joy." This process in the psychological literature is referred to as "idealizing and mirroring," or "ascent and descent." Mary represents the vessel within us, containing the virgin healing energies open to the transcendent power which can make our "impossibilities" realities. Mary at the annunciation represents in us the new creation and the possibility of recovering joy, and through an awareness of joy to experience a greater capacity to love.

Whatever one's religious persuasion one cannot help being touched by the poetry of the Hebrew and Christian biblical Advent texts. The Advent liturgy offers a rich fare of images: images of death and destruction, images of hope, of struggle, of waiting, of pain, puzzlement, questioning, doubt, images of birth and of love. Psychologically speaking, it is more important to experience an image than to interpret it or to relate it to mythological sources, helpful though this may be. Experiencing opens us to the energizing power of the image which "feeds" us, giving us substance and meaning. Whether the image comes from the Bible, Koran, I Ching, Tarot, or from our dreams and visions, the image brings us in touch with a wisdom and shared experience of humanity. Images of Advent speak to us of our yearning for life, even as the One whose birth we celebrate came to give us life "to the full."

Probably no other time of the year evokes in us such a

range of emotional response—from sadness to joy—as the weeks leading up to the feast of Christmas. The word, "Advent," from the Latin, *adventus,* means "coming" or "approach." The word connotes a longing or hunger for something more in life, something intimated but still unfelt. For Christians this longing focuses on the divine child, a child who was embodied in the Jesus of history, and who, from a psychological perspective relates us to "unborn" aspects of ourselves. Advent, then, is the season of the unborn. And it is this aspect of Advent that we will explore as images of psychic pregnancy and birth. Each of us nurtures some promise that wants to be born. Psychic birth refers to any potential aspect of ourselves that longs for realization; it refers to our "becoming" who we are meant to be.

Advent biblical imagery metaphors the individuation process, the reconciliation and balancing of opposites within the personality, the conscious and the unconscious. Ideally the ego holds the tension between the two sides dialoguing and integrating aspects of the "dark unknown." This may happen, for example when our intellectual development dwarfs our feeling and emotional life, causing, perhaps, neurosis and psychosomatic symptoms. The "new" possibility, the more balanced personality may be symbolized through a reconciling symbol. The child is such a unifying symbol, born of two opposites, masculine and feminine, conscious and unconscious.

But what happens when the ego is not strong enough to stand the tension of opposites when, for example, the feeling or instinctual side has been so repressed that a healthy tension of opposites does not exist? This may be due to a poor "fit" between mother and infant through the fault of neither, or it may be due to emotional and bodily absence of a nurturing adult. In a letter to Walter Corti Jung wrote that God wants to be born in the flame of our consciousness.

But we must be strong enough to bear this flame. And what if this flame has no roots in the earth? "Could God then be born? One must be able to suffer God."[4] In Jung's view God becomes conscious through each of us. We are God's limitation in time and space. In striving to find our own self, we become an "earthly tabernacle" for God. When this becomes our path toward psychic growth, then the pattern of ego development becomes the pattern of individuation. In these pages my focus on psychic birth refers primarily to this development. The divine child, then, might refer not only to God but also to the hidden "cut-off" sense of self, the ego identity. But the Advent message brings healing as we resonate to its themes of death and birth out of our deepest need. Whether our need is to become more "grounded" in our "earth," that is, in our own ego self, whether our need is for liberation from the pull of opposite tensions in our life, or whether our need is simply one for renewal and affirmation of God's presence within us, the Advent imagery can speak to us in a deeply personal way.

In linking God's incarnation in Jesus and our own personal "becoming," the biblical imagery of Advent leads us into the depths of our own hope, desire, and joy. To awaken Advent within us means to open ourselves to the call to be initiated more fully into the meaning of death and birth, that mythic reality that fires our longing to experience the Life dwelling within us. During Advent the child carries that image of Life in all its various meanings. It evokes first the image of Jesus as divine child, a child-god. On a human level it recalls our own childhood as well as the child side of ourselves always present. On another level this Life is related to the "child motif," the mythological and symbolical child. In his *Psychology of the Child Archetype* Jung writes that this image of child links us to our own preconscious past, to our psychic roots, for the child lived a psychic life before it became conscious. The image of child, then, links us to our origins. Symbolically the child motif also links us to the future, because the child represents potential; it wants to develop. While the child links us to the past, it never ceases to look forward.

In tracing the psychic roots of Advent we come to see the deeper meaning of the recurrent celebration of Christmas, bringing before us again and again through ritual repetition of the mythical event the link to our origins, so that this link with our original condition may not be broken. For when we lose our relation to the instinctive side of the unconscious we become unchildlike and artificial. Unrelated to these vital energies within we begin to suffer from a sense of emptiness. Could it be that this separation from our inner "fire" may account in some way for the depressive symptoms so often suffered during the Advent-Christmas season? Are these symptoms caused by the physical and psychic effects of sunlessness? We know that during the weeks before Christmas many people feel more anxious, restless, irritable, and even hostile. Clinically we refer to this phenomenon as the "holiday syndrome." Above all, there is often loneliness, experienced more poignantly amidst Christmas partying. At times the outer celebrations find little resonance within. Perhaps it is within this very dissonance that we can discover the psychic roots of Advent, as a way leading us back to our instinctive roots, to the child.

This child is also a symbol of hope, and hope is linked with our heartfelt desire to risk the new and to create the new. The child envisions possibilities and opens its heart to them. A child cannot will otherwise. What can we say, then, about the sense of hopelessness that weighs on so many of us, or about depression, suicide, addiction, and the poverty of spirit historian Christopher Lasch points to as the sign of an unhealthy narcissism pervading our culture?[5] Maybe we can get some light on these questions by asking another. Is it possible that out of our very poverty of spirit hope re-awakens, hope as a catalyst of desire?

Advent stirs up that deepest desire in us symbolized by the child—the urge to realize our true self. We live in an age that abuses, victimizes and neglects children, and this in itself reflects the need we have as adults to give attention to the side of us which, perhaps, has suffered the same fate. The "self-pathologies" of our time, especially narcissism or self-hate has reached epidemic proportions. This means that many children grow to adulthood with either a grandiose or deflated self-image that defends against both the vulnerable as well as the powerful hidden self and causes untold heartache, self-destructive activity, and waste of human potential.

Many years ago Jung wrote that the tragedy we face today results from our uprooting from grounding in the unconscious, or we might say, in Mother Earth. All that follows from that—psychosomatic illness, spiritual malaise, wounded self-esteem—we know well. While Jung always expressed interest in the historical cause of physical or psychic problems, he felt that we must also ask: What is the purpose of this disturbance? To what does it call attention? Can we discover the hidden value in it? Can we ask, "What is God calling me to in this depression?" Can we say, for example, that the prevalence of a sense of emptiness and loneliness in our society points to a collective hunger, not only for those aspects of our personality that want to be freed, but for the emergence of a hidden self? The value of this disturbance, then, may lie in its opening us to an awareness of our hunger for God and self, two aspects of the same reality.

It is failure to live our individual pattern that leads to a sense of emptiness and loneliness. This feeling is heightened in those who have been forced to abandon their own instinctive life with its needs and desires. "False self" is Donald Winnicott's phrase which describes a person who, out of need for survival in childhood, became compliant to the wishes and demands of others, and thus lost contact with his or her instinctive needs. This condition sometimes results in a feeling of being cut off from others, unrecognized, unable to communicate what is of deepest importance. Describing such a person, psychologist Stephen Kurtz writes of T.S. Eliot, that as a child he suffered isolation which left its scars of fragmentation. Eliot, it seems, was an unexpected child of middle-aged parents. One sister was eight years old when he was born; another was away at college. Eliot's father was growing deaf and was emotionally distant. Kurtz and Edel suggest that Eliot's mother projected on him her own need to be praised and acknowledged for literary achievement and that she treated him as a late "gift of God." Eliot's precociousness was reinforced by certain physical ailments, in particular a hernia which kept him from sports.[6] Eliot's mother did not raise the child but entrusted him to the care of an Irish nurse. This pattern is well known to therapists who note that the real child often was never seen, although his or her parents may have provided material care and goods. The child as idealized projection of parents' needs is treated as special and "a little god" but the real child hides in isolation, emotionally alone and neglected, perhaps only to realize much later that he or she was never loved and never had a childhood. Psychologically there are many variations on this theme, and the problems many experience today getting in touch with feelings and needs often stem from unmet needs for holding, mirroring, and understanding. When parents idealize their children, they fail to love the whole child, "the child of vomit, shit, fear and rage."[7] The child is rewarded for "proper" behavior, cleanness, and intellectual accomplishment. When this happens the child comes to loathe his "dirty self" the real self. Lack of self-esteem begins very early.

Like many therapists, I have heard people say, "I don't have a self. I fluctuate. If I'm praised I have one, if I'm neglected or criticized, I lose it." A woman I knew dreamed she had been born on another planet. She said, "Maybe that explains why I feel that I don't belong here. I don't feel that I'm *in* my life." Even the desire to be "incarnated" or reconnected with instinctual needs and wants seems to go underground. Eliot, in *The Waste Land* writes of this sense of imprisonment:

> We think of the key, each in his prison
> Thinking of the key, each confirms a prison[8]

The message of Advent speaks to this sense of imprisonment and isolation. Advent's darkness is related to the depressive's suffering in which despair seems to stifle hope.

Yet Advent's night closely resembles the mystic's night of the soul, that is, a felt absence yet a sense that Life is there in the darkness. It is as if in the darkness hides another "key" that opens the prison. As part of a series of cries for freedom which we will reflect on later, one of the Advent "O" Antiphons captures a response to Eliot's verse. It is the antiphon read during the fourth week of Advent.

> O key of David, O royal Power of Israel, controlling at your will the gate of heaven (Isaiah 22:22); come, break down the prison walls of death for those who dwell in darkness and the shadow of death; and lead your captive people into freedom (Isaiah 42:7).[9]

Keys are associated with initiation and with the mysteries. In alchemy the goal or the "lapis" was referred to as "key."[10] And significantly, in ancient Egypt the key was associated with the cross. The gods often held the "Nem Ankh," the cross of eternal life, by the top as if it were a key. It was used in ceremonies of the dead in order to open the gates of death into immortality.

It seems that Eliot himself found this key through discovering his creative gift. In poetry he communicated his own longing and, touching depths in his readers, opened them to the "hints" and "guesses" of a deeper source of freedom. After his own experience of the wilderness, Eliot discovered that out of the wounding comes a gift that links us to a source of freedom that would otherwise, perhaps, have remained closed. This is the paradox of Advent in its darkness-light symbolism. Advent darkness stirs up, on the one hand, unconscious fears and, on the other, a deep desire for freedom and for all that the child represents. Fear of consciousness and rebirth is the fear of change, and for most of us, nothing is so feared as the prospect of moving into the dark, but that is often where the key is to be found.

Advent as an initiatory journey from darkness to light celebrates the hidden "sun" and the hidden self waiting to be born. In the words of a traditional Christmas hymn the divine child "bloomed" like a rose in the cold of a winter midnight. The qualities associated with the rose: love, virginity, fertility, passion and eros, appear only intermittently in the imagery of Advent. It is as if they, too, are hidden like the new sun of the winter solstice. But we know that they are as present there as is the birth we await.

1

Anticipation

When we anticipate something we look forward to a future that we can imagine, a new possibility. And in our anticipating we often experience a foretaste of the event we fantasize. It is as if our hunger were already being appeased. Something of the excitement of anticipation flavors the whole of the Advent season even though, from its inauguration in Rome in A.D. 336 its tone combined, along with a joyous air of expectancy, a somber penitential spirit. Both of these strains were influenced by the winter solstice festivals. In this chapter we shall look at some rituals and practices of these New Year's festivals with attention to the underlying myth of eternal return in its relation to the rebirth of the seasons and its reenactment at the festivals. We shall then look at the myth as it relates to our own anticipation of psychic birth.

These festivals had been celebrated for centuries along with prayers and rituals to petition the gods and goddesses of fertility to send back the sun to a dark, cold, sterile land. Just like our own Advent and Christmas, the festivals had to be celebrated every year, for they were more than commemorations. The festivals restored hope; they turned things around and enabled life, symbolized by the "return" of the sun, to begin again. Infusing all the festive activities was a joyfully exuberant expectation that the old year or sun having "died," the new would, as a result of each person's sacrifice and participation in the ritual, inevitably reappear.

Unless we have lived in the northern hemisphere, it is difficult for us to imagine life lived in darkness for long stretches of time. Such living must have intensified an awareness of dependency on the sun and a longing for its return. But as the cycles of the seasons and the years repeated themselves, the people perhaps anticipated the new with pleasurable expectation in the midst of their festive activity. But as we know, anticipation can stir quietly, too; for example, when we sit silently at dawn waiting for the sun to appear. For often something arises within us, too, as if from another realm not of our making. Can something be anticipated that we have not seen or felt before? This is a question people in therapy sometimes ask. How can a "sun" rise in my inner landscape when there seems to be nothing but darkness? It would seem that the ancients, in celebrating the underlying myth of their festivals, touched on this human dilemma. Myths express the meaning of life because they are woven into its fabric. The myth of eternal return moves us to act out the eternal drama of life "falling apart," returning to chaos or the time before time began, to reorder or re-create itself. But the myth also states, like the book of Genesis, that something can be created out of what is experienced as a "void."

The winter solstice festivals of old, like all festivals, represent a kind of revolution. They turn things around and enable us to start again by going back to a moment pregnant with new possibilities. We shall look at this idea in more detail in the following pages. In some ways our own yearly celebration of Advent and Christmas is less "charged" with this awareness of the possibility of rebirth and change.

No doubt this is so because during the season of Advent we commemorate a unique event in history, the birth of Christ. Christians believe that the incarnation of the Son of God sanctifies history, making it meaningful, "infusing" it with the divine. Christ's birth and death are not repeatable; Christ died once and for all to bring salvation (1 Peter 3:18). In contrast, the gods of the cyclical religions "die" and are "reborn" according to the rhythm of the seasons; for example, as the sun "dies" at the winter solstice and is "reborn." Christianity has been influenced by the cyclical religions, not only in the dating of its feasts, but in its theology and liturgical practice.[1] In the east, for example, Epiphany and later Christmas, were celebrated on January 6th, previously the date of a pagan winter solstice festival. And in the west December 25th was chosen to celebrate the birthday of Jesus, because it corresponded to the observance of the Mithraic birth of the sun god. By choosing these dates the church wished to counteract the influence of the god, Mithras, by proclaiming Christ as the *true* sun, born into history.

Even though Christianity has been influenced by the myths of the cyclical religions, it is probably true to say that most Christians today do not readily make connections between the central dogmas of their belief and these myths. Theologian Harvey Cox alludes to some reasons for this lack when he contrasts historical and non-historical religions. He writes that cosmic religions like Tibetan Buddhism focus on recurrents in life and nature. "They help us to situate ourselves in the larger cosmic setting."[2] On the other hand, historical religions spring from particular events—the Exodus or the birth and death of Christ—and their festivals celebrate these events. Cox concludes that while we have learned the importance of history from our religion, "we have now lost our religion and are left only with history."[3] Today these words seem less shocking than they were for many in 1969 when Cox wrote them. Years earlier Jung had written that we are living through a crisis of soul because our religion has been reduced to externals; we have, he said, lost connection to the psyche and to the myths which pattern and feed its life. Let us turn now to one of these myths as it was relived in the winter festivals of old and at the "death-rebirth" of each season. It is a myth that restored hope then and it is the myth underlying the death-rebirth symbolism of the Advent season.

For our early ancestors each season was a time of renewal or rebirth. Before the concept of "year" as a measure of time existed, these people used to determine time in rather vague periods, such as when the crops had to be sown or reaped, or when the moon waxed or waned, or when the flowers appeared or the leaves died. These shorter spans of time then combined into longer ones such as seasons of heat or cold, of rainfall and drought. The Eskimos of Greenland, for example, recognized only the season of winter; the Seminole Indians of Florida recognized only summer and the time in-between was considered "dead" or unaccounted for.[4] At this time the seasons did not make up a continuous year.

That "primitive" people measured time by seasons was apparent from the fact that the word "year" for some meant "springtime." In the ancient Sanskrit of India "year" originally meant "autumn."[5] Gradually people began to attach seasons astronomically to signs, the position of the sun, moon and stars. Spring was recognized with the rising of the Pleiades and winter became the logical time of beginnings or New Year because the sun began to increase in strength. Until as late as the eighteenth century, however, the vernal equinox or March 25th was generally regarded as New Year's Day. This explains why we see vestiges of the winter solstice festivals such as the lighting of fire, initiations, retelling of the creation myth, during the present day Christian Easter liturgy. This shows that the old concept of seasons as beginnings "retain their hold as crucial moments in the life of the world."[6]

These times are crucial because in our ancestors' view life is not one progression from birth to death. There are moments of death-renewal, times of initiation when we must reconnect to the timeless, before creation began, and in doing this we ourselves can be re-created. Another way of expressing this idea is to say that as each season ended it was as if the lease had run out and had to be renewed. The renewal was not automatic. For example, if the sun had "disappeared" at the winter solstice, it would not return automatically, so to speak, but each person had to help make it return through his or her own efforts. Our ancestors felt involved with the gods in this effort. This interaction with the gods is reminiscent of a conversation with a Pueblo Indian that Jung recounts in his autobiography.

Jung wrote that in his travels to America he talked to a Pueblo Indian who spoke with excitement about how his religion benefited the whole world. On closer questioning by Jung, the man replied:

> We are the people who live on the roof of the world; we are the sons of the Father Sun, and with our religion we daily help our father to go across the sky. We do this not only for ourselves, but for the whole world. If we were to cease practicing our religion, in ten years the sun would no longer rise. Then it would be night forever.[7]

Jung reflects on what might seem to a sophisticated westerner as the naïveté of the Indian in contrast to our cleverness. But this so-called cleverness is really a cloak for our own impoverishment, for the Indian's dignity is based on a metaphysical factor. He and God regulate the life of the world; his life is meaningful because he is at home in the mythic world and has found his place. "Knowledge," writes Jung, "does not enrich us if it removes us more and more from the mythic world in which we were once at home by right of birth."[8]

It is this pattern of the daily journey of the sun through its "sleep" in darkness to its birth as a new day that is writ large in the myth of eternal return. Now let us look at this myth which forms the basis of the oldest record we have of a New Year ritual. Saturnalia festivals were part of the early Babylonian New Year, and these were later celebrated at Rome and throughout the European world. If people failed to participate in the festival there would be no rebirth. For ancient peoples the word "year" came to be interchangeable with cosmos or world. The world, then, was "born," "lived," and "died." For the world to be reborn it must return to the "original" time, to the origins before creation; psychologically speaking, to the realm of the archetypes. Between the death and the re-creation of the world it was necessary to pass through a period of chaos. Chaos is a prerequisite for reestablishing life and order. This pattern we will meet again in the alchemical symbolism and, as well, in the Advent biblical texts. It is the cyclical pattern of nature and of life.

The myth of cyclic time is found, not only in relation to fertility rituals, but also in preagricultural societies. Our ancestors probably observed the moon, for the moon was the first measure of time. Moon rhythm begins with "birth," or the "new moon" followed by growth to the full moon, and then its "death" or waning; a "death" followed by three moonless nights. This image of birth, growth, death, rebirth helped archaic peoples to crystallize this view of the cosmogonic myth of periodic death and re-creation of the world and of the year. The world, the year, time itself grows weary and grows old. How does time get regenerated? It must return to the origins, to sacred time when the gods first created, the *illud tempore* in which the world first came into existence. By participating ritually in the end of the world and its re-creation, for example, through the winter solstice festivals, it became possible for each person to be "present," as it were, with this "original" or time before time, the archetypal source out of which time began.

Eliade explains that for our archaic ancestors it was only by participating in this original act of the gods' creation that everyday actions and objects achieve value. They can be born anew and begin life over because they have touched the vital energies present at the moment of birth. They become "real" because they participate in a transcendent reality.[9] Eliade cites Iranian cosmology to show what he means when he says that each human action participates in this transcendence. In this way of viewing the world everything in life, whether concrete or abstract, corresponds to a heavenly or transcendent "idea" in the Platonic sense. Our sky corresponds to an invisible "sky." Our earth corresponds to a celestial earth, and so on.[10] In this system our human actions achieve value when they repeat the gods' action at the beginning of time. Every birth, or marriage, every building of a city, or a house, every installation of a ruler, all participate in the original creative activity of the gods. Even wild uncultivated regions in chaos participate in the modality of precreation. By reciting the myths and stories of creation, creation begins anew in the here and now.

The reenactment of the myth and the winter solstice festivals form part of a larger ritual where the death and resurrection of the god of fertility was dramatized. In Mesopotamia the New Year's festival began with a ritual in the temple, symbolically, the "center of the world," the place of new energy. The high priest would enter the temple before dawn and would unveil a picture of the mythological god, Marduk, who, in the old days had created the earth from the remains of the sea monster, Tiamat, whom he had conquered. This struggle and victory symbolized the power of the god over all adversaries. Next, god and goddess were addressed as the restorers of order, though the new order is not restored until the Saturnalia festival has been celebrated.

Five elements are central to this festival: a period of purification, confession and fasting, the symbolic "death" of the king, the return of the dead followed by a period of upheaval and chaos, and, finally, restoration of order and the beginning of a new life symbolized by the birth of a child. Between the first part of the ritual, reenactment of the myth, and the birth of the child from the reunited king and queen, there was a period of topsy-turveyness and chaos. Indeed, the birth of the child and restoration come only through the experience of chaos.

Now let us look in some detail at the elements of Saturnalia; first, at the king. In the earliest records of history the king was regarded as a kind of god. He was responsible for the well-being of society because he stabilized life and gave "soul" to each member of the community. If a king became ill or impotent, he had to be replaced by a healthy king. Only then could the fertility of the land and the prosperity of the tribe be assured. When the life of the culture wore down, when the spirit waned, this signified a need for a new king. In primitive societies the king was often "killed" in effigy as part of the New Year's festival. This death ritual was accompanied by a spirit of mortification among the people. They fasted and performed other austerities at this time of year to represent their own "dying" spirit and the "death" of the sun and of vegetation. This dying signifies hope, for Saturnalia is a fertility festival; Saturn is the god of the seed. As the king "dies," so the seed "dies" in the earth inviting sun and rain to warm and nourish it into life.

Dying represented a letting go of old worn-out structures and supports. These had to be mixed up and "ground down," as it were, to the *prima materia*. Saturnalia dramatized this mix-up. During the days leading up to December 25th all hierarchical rule—and class—were suspended. Servants sat at table with their masters; all drank good wine and exchanged gifts. During this time gambling was allowed and all debts were written off. Resentments and angry outbursts were contrary to the spirit of the feast. One of the remarkable features of the Saturnalia festival was the mingling of all social classes in a kind of Dionysian revelry. The tone of this gathering may be glimpsed from a fragment by the writer Lucian:

> The festivals were marked by drinking and being drunk, noise and games and dice, appointing of kings and feasting of slaves, singing naked, clapping of tremulous hands, an occasional ducking of corked faces in icy waters . . .[11]

Records show that during this time men dressed in women's clothes; women dressed in men's clothes. All rules of "proper" sexual behavior were suspended. The sexual orgies prominent at this time were part of a ritual of petition to the gods for a good harvest. In ancient times it was thought that ritual sexual activity actually increased the earth's fertility.

To add to the general chaos, or return to primordial beginnings, the dead were said to return to take part in the festivities. The dead must be present to complete the gathering of all people and to establish equality among them. We speak sometimes about the dead being with us in spirit. But during these festivals the dead were believed to be really present. There are traces of this belief in the practices of our Halloween, a tradition that goes back to the ancient Celtic New Year celebrations at the beginning of winter.[12] The ancient Babylonians believed that the dead participated in the New Year's festivals, and food was set out for them. At the opening of the year, the Romans used to celebrate a nine-day festival of Parentalia, or Departed Ancestors.

Many ancient peoples—the Babylonians, Persians, Romans—celebrated the return of the dead during the New Year's celebrations. Today, among the Siamese, the dead are thought to rejoin their families at the New Year, which is celebrated in April. During their summer solstice festival, the Hopi Indians believe the dead return to participate in the village activities. Dead ancestors in the Ukraine are said to return at Easter and Christmas. The people pray, "O God, let all the dead and all the lost come back and drink with us."[13] After the ceremonies prayer is offered for the living, peace is made with the dead and their spirits depart. There is something very profound in this practice. When the New Year or new life begins, it begins with the presence and energy from the past, that is, the past is part of the present, living with and within us.

Eliade sees the December Saturnalia festival, with its overturn of rule and order, its sexual excess and the return of the dead as central to the myth of "eternal return," the return to beginnings.

> How could the invasion by the souls of the dead be anything but the sign of a suspension of profane time, the paradoxical realization of a co-existence of "past" and

"present"? This co-existence is never so complete as at a period of chaos when all modalities coincide. The last days of the year can be identified with the pre-Creation chaos, both through this invasion of the dead—which annuls the law of time—and through sexual excesses which commonly mark the occasion. Even if, as the result of successive calendar reforms, the Saturnalia finally no longer coincided with the end and the beginning of the year, they nevertheless continued to mark the abolitions of all norms and, in their violence, to illustrate an overturning of values.[14]

Before turning to the psychological implications of the restoration of the king and the return of the dead, let us mention other distinctive features of the winter solstice festivals which helped to break down barriers between the social classes. Of greatest importance was feasting; people shared food and gifts.

While special foods were prepared and left outside the door for the "spirits" or "ghosts" who returned at this time, it is the living who gathered around the hearth, sharing and rejoicing in the coming new year. Suggestions were given for gifts exchanged between the rich and the poor. If the poor were learned, they were encouraged to write a story or poem, but the unlearned were to send "a garland or grains of frankincense."[15] As for food, people were encouraged to give in to their impulse toward extravagance:

Everywhere may be seen carousals and well-laden tables; luxurious abundance is found in the houses of the rich, but also in houses of the poor better food than usual is put on the table. The impulse to spend seizes everyone . . . a stream of presents pours itself out on all sides . . . Another great quality of the festival is that it teaches men not to hold too fast to their money, but to part with it and let it pass into other hands.[16]

We note here how Saturnalia, as part of the celebration of the myth of return to the origins, begins with fasting and mortification and concludes with feasting, gift-giving and general merrymaking. The final stage of the New Year's festival comes with the sacred marriage of the king and queen and the birth of the child, represented in our times as the New Year's babe or the image of renewed time.

We have outlined the basic elements present in the myth of eternal return with emphasis on the Saturnalia. Our ancestors reenacted the myth at the beginning of the year or season, or at the installation of a new leader. They also made use of the creation myth as a therapeutic method. It was believed that if the ill person could return to the past, he or she could live again at the "moment" of creation and experience the fullness of energies, out of which a new birth would come. In archaic thought the cure is to go back and repeat the birth. Psychologically, to return through memory to the past is not only to return to childhood but also to the collective unconscious, those psychic structures within us that precede our individual existence. "The essential human condition precedes the actual human condition. That decisive deed took place before us, and even before our parents; that decisive deed having been done by the mythic ancestor."[17] Whether we regard the "return" as movement back to the Ancestor, in the Judeo-Christian context, Adam, or whether we speak of archetypes, we need to confront, repeat, or relive the drama of these energies within us. The return is made to enable us to move into the future, and during this journey we experience aspects of the creation myth: death of the old king, darkness and chaos, the "return" of the dead, and the joy of rebirth.

How can we view these aspects as energies within ourselves? What would the old king represent? As we have seen, in early societies the king was regarded as the "soul" of the people, giving vitality to the culture because he represented the political and religious structures of the culture. Today in societies where the government no longer works for the people, or where churches seem out of touch with the "soul" needs of the people, we can say that the "king" is getting old and weary and needs to be replaced. In ourselves, when we feel worn out, unrelated to the vital energies within, we can say the "king" is old. But as the "king" grows old he often becomes set in his ways. As King Herod feared the birth of the new king, Christ, so do we often fear the new because it means letting go of the old. But the "dead" or repressed call us back to life. If in our life, for example, we have lost touch with our instinctual needs and desires, we are called to return to the source of creation, to rediscover the imprisoned "child." Whatever in us calls for healing and restoration leads us back to the ancestors, to our inner solstice drama where the "dead," like the seed, may be honored as the carrier of new life.

In Christian tradition the "cult of the dead" corresponded with an earlier festival beginning on November 1st, the Celtic New Year. On November 1st the dead who had been recognized as saints were honored, and later the custom developed of honoring all the dead by offering masses on November 2nd, which came to be called All Souls' Day. But in early Christianity pagan beliefs persisted, along with the developing Christian ritual of remembering the dead. In ancient Greece, for example, during November pots were placed in the kitchen near the fire. The pots represented the womb of the earth or the underworld, and they contained corn seeds symbolizing the dead, or "ghosts." They were said to belong to Demeter as Earth Goddess, and as such, they held the secret of life. It became evident that people at this time were not satisfied honoring the dead

only with the mass. The dead were still considered as present and had to be taken seriously.

Jung once described a fantasy in which his soul or life
energy seemed to leave him and he felt depressed. He interpreted this as his soul going into the "land of the dead, the
ancestors," that is, withdrawing into the unconscious which
became like a medium

> giving the dead a chance to manifest themselves, ani-
> mating them . . . from that time on the dead have be-
> come ever more distinct for me as the voices of the
> Unanswered, Unresolved, and Unredeemed; for since
> my questions and demands which my destiny required
> me to answer did not come to me from outside they
> must have come from the inner world.[18]

These inner unredeemed voices are, like grains of wheat,
waiting to spring into life; they are the soul of the ancestors,
e.g., talents, possibilities which we have inherited, and they
wait in the unconscious to begin to live. These voices may
also be viewed as shadow envy and rage, the repressed
"dead" which are potentially transformable if consciously
recognized and experienced and then channeled through
creative activity. Like the hidden sun celebrated during the
New Year fertility festivals, the dead are linked with a creative divinity who wishes to be awakened.

As we come in touch with these "ancestors" we will
begin to experience some of the chaos represented in Saturnalia as the revelry and "leveling" begins to stir from within.
From a psychological perspective one way of viewing this
shaking up of old patterns is to see it through the image of
the trickster. Jung writes that the trickster is an archetypal
energy personified in a kind of devilish figure who likes to
mix things up. The trickster plays jokes and tries to get us to

see things in a different light. He shakes up patterns that may have grown rigid so that they may be re-formed. The trickster reverses social hierarchies, structures that repress shadow energies. The trickster says, "Look at the other side," "What if. ..." "Just because you have always lived this way does not mean . . ." When we return to the "origins," psychologically we experience a "topsy-turveyness" as old attitudes are challenged. In the therapeutic process such a "turning around" is needed to make right what has been damaged in early childhood. The word therapy itself connotes a turning around or upside down. Often through the confusion of our turnings, hope emerges.

Festivals feed hope. They proclaim, as does the Advent mystery of annunciation, that even in the face of seeming impossibility and hopelessness, hope may appear as a new birth. From a psychological perspective this birth represents the dawning of consciousness and the emergence of aspects of ourselves never experienced before. In his book, *Holding and Interpretation,* Donald Winnicott records the words of one of his patients who

> wondered how there could be hope of getting at some-
> thing here in the analysis which had never been before.
> "Is it possible to get at something in one's nature that
> does not yet 'exist?' How can one achieve concern when
> it has never been there before? Can something be cre-
> ated out of nothing? . . . Is there something buried which
> can be discovered?"[19]

This analysand asks not only whether something psychically "dead" or repressed can begin to live, but whether something unfelt or "non-existent" in oneself can be discovered. This man had perhaps for so long conformed to unemotional ways of responding that he began to feel

empty, to feel that life was not worth living. He asks not
about rebirth and rejuvenation, but whether something can
be "born" from a sense of "nothingness." Our ancestors
evoked the cosmic myth of death-rebirth whenever the
world or the year was "wearing out." Entering pre-creation
"time" or the archetypal world opened the possibility for
re-creation. There are hints, too, that life can be "created"
out of "no-thing."

Eliade cites a Polynesian creation myth in which there
is only cosmic darkness. From "within the breathing space
of immensity" Io, the supreme god, emerged. Then light
appeared. "Ye water of Tai-Kama, be ye separate. Heaven,
be formed!" Recalling these ancient words of wisdom which
caused growth from the void, one Polynesian writer recalls
that the myth was applied in a ritual "for planting a child in
the barren womb."[20] Can we say that the myths express the
profound truth revealed again in the virgin birth that something can be born from the "void" within us, something that
emerges as our own felt reality and substance? From the
viewpoint of depth psychology this means that a sudden
movement from the unconscious can stir up life, that our
psyche is capable of *creatio ex nihilo*.

The underlying myth of Advent shares in the meaning
of the cosmogonic myth both in the sense of renewal and
new creation. It is no coincidence that initiations in some
ritual form were always part of the older New Year's celebrations. And we find remnants of this in the rites of initiation making up part of the Holy Saturday service in the
Catholic liturgy. Before the Julian reform of the calendar, as
we have noted, New Year was celebrated at the vernal equinox on March 25th. Both the initiatory rite of baptism and
the reading of the creation myth are meant to make present
the "time before creation" when all can be born anew. Psychologically viewed this Easter rite celebrating Christ's vic-

tory over death can symbolize the transformation of the ego, of a life lived in relation to the Self. Advent, on the other hand, can symbolize the birth of the ego or of the real self, and this psychic birth is related to God's birth in us. In both Easter and Advent we are initiated into the mystery of life through death. Baptism itself is part of the lenten ritual, though the Baptist himself figures prominently in the Advent liturgy.

Advent is a feminine mystery. The child born of Mary is Jesus, called the Christ. Our psychic "child" is born through a "return to the origins" or the "womb" of the unconscious. This Advent longing for rebirth or birth is beautifully expressed in this poem by Anne Sexton:

> Oh, Mary
> Gentle Mother,
> open the door and let me in.
> A bee has stung your belly with faith.
> Let me float in it like a fish.
> Let me in! Let me in!
> I have been born many times, a false Messiah,
> but let me be born again
> into something true.[21]

This imagery reminds us of a matriarchal time when the Earth Goddess gave birth to all living creatures from herself without the help of the male, for the bee is an image of virginity and parthenogenic birth. In this poem the speaker has had enough of falseness and wants to be born into something "true." The birth comes from the belly of "faith." It is faith that carries us out of the "void" or the seemingly hopeless situation, faith in the Christian sense that God, indeed, works miracles, and faith as the stuff of fairy tales, the "magic" that accomplishes the impossible, whether it means climbing the glass mountain or finding the ring at the bottom of the ocean. Psychologically speaking, help comes from the unconscious, the unknown source of life within, the regenerative womb.

We have only remnants of a Saturnalia festival honoring the moon goddess who would re-create the world from her own being through her sun or moon "child." In Greece, Demeter as Earth Goddess was honored as holding the secret of life imaged in the seed. In these cultures where Mother Earth was honored, the seed was imaged as a vulva ready to sprout new life.[22] Historically, the feminine carries the possibility of renewal as it comes into birth. It is this source of rejuvenation that calls us through our longing to enter and to be reborn "true" to our own self.

In summary, we have seen that the winter solstice festivals form one part of a larger mythic pattern of renewal through return to the "origins." The creation story was acted out in the temple, followed by the ritual death of the old or dying king. Following this "return" to pre-creation, a marriage took place between the king and queen or the god and goddess. The birth of a child symbolized the New Year and the rebirth of the cosmos. Between the death of the king and the appearance of the new king, chaos reigned with the mixing of classes and roles, the return of the "dead," and general revelry. Psychologically, the path toward psychic birth follows this pattern.

During Advent we anticipate the coming of Jesus as divine child. If this anticipation is not to be merely a commemoration we, like our ancestors, can celebrate the death of the old as well as the recovery of the "dead" within ourselves that wants to live again. Advent evokes the myth of eternal return which, psychologically viewed, is a return to the feminine from which all birth comes. It is from there that we may be born into "something true." Mary as Virgin represents the Mother of the Living, and the unconscious, or "origins." From these origins comes new life out of the darkness, out of impossibility and "death." Let us now trace some patterns of rebirth in the earth creation myths and the alchemical *opus,* for these, too, offer us metaphors of the Advent mystery, and, as well, of our own longing for rebirth.

"The Annunciation" by Fra Angelico (Prado, Madrid). On the left
Adam and Eve are shown leaving Paradise. Mary, as Immaculate Conception and Virgin, represents "time before time" and the possibility of
a new creation. (Courtesy Alinari/Art Resource, NY.)

2

Longing

Winter slows us down, drawing us inward where, if we resist the pull to be in constant motion, we feel our longing. We carry within us, as the myth of eternal return mirrors for us, a sense of lack which we cannot blame on anyone. This sense that we are lacking in some way is archetypal, a part of our human condition. We are dissatisfied with our fragmentation and scatteredness and we long for "at-one-ment" or union with something or someone "Other." Our early ancestors celebrated this longing in the "death and resurrection" of the sun and of all vegetation at the New Year's festivals. In world mythologies death was viewed as a new beginning, and the return of the dead at Saturnalia represented possibilities for renewed life and the awakening of hidden potential.

In this chapter we want to view longing as it was expressed by another group of our ancestors, the medieval alchemists, and to relate the pattern of their *opus* to the longing inherent in our own life and mirrored in the Advent imagery. The medieval alchemists, forerunners of modern chemistry, saw this pattern of death-life in the process they called the *opus,* the work of transforming earth or the heaviness of lead into light or into "gold." Jung was attracted to alchemy because he saw in it an historical pattern which paralleled his theory of individuation, the "becoming" of the human personality, a personality that comes to wholeness through the union of opposites—the base and the noble, the light and the dark. The "gold" according to the alchemists, is found in the lowest, most despised aspects of matter. Though the alchemists may not have expressed it this way, we might say that something valuable and life-giving comes from where we least expect it. According to the cosmogonic myth cited earlier, the gold as a sense of self comes not only from the experience of a vulnerable side of ourselves but even out of our sense of nothingness or emptiness. As we recall, the creation myth was read as part of a ritual for birth, or for "placing the child in a barren womb." The alchemists viewed the goal of their process as a birth, as new life coming out of the darkness and chaos, the blackness of *nigredo*.

The images found in Advent and in alchemy pattern for us a "way" toward our goal of psychic birth, sharing, as they do, a central image of pregnancy and birth. In Christianity, this birth comes from above: "Oh, that you would tear the heavens open and come down!" (Isaiah 64:1). In alchemy the birth comes from below, from the earth. During Advent Christians "wait" for the birth of Jesus, the true sun. In alchemy the goal is called son, gold, child, "lapis" or stone. All of these refer to a quality within us, a healing immortal and indestructible quality. Jung compared the lapis to Christ. Advent and the alchemical *opus* begin in darkness, progressing gradually into light. From the Advent darkness emerges the Baptist, who calls into the wilderness, a deeper darkness. Only by the fourth week of the Advent liturgy does dawn appear heralding the angel's greeting to Mary at whose *fiat* life begins to stir. Similarly the alchemical *opus* begins in *nigredo,* passes through its own wilderness of suffering and into the brightness of dawn where the child or gold is experienced. Both Advent and alchemy celebrate the mystery of the feminine, of earth, and of matter, though the medieval alchemists intuited more strongly than many Christians of their time the need for experiencing this mystery in a personal way. Alchemy reflects the universal belief expressed in many creation myths that human beings are born from the depths of the earth. Before looking in more detail at the alchemists and their *opus* as it relates to the Advent imagery, let us look at some of these early creation myths.

A number of the creation myths speak of the preexistence of the human race within the "bowels" of the earth. Our ancestors believed that the Great Mother keeps mankind in her body until they are ready to live "in the world." Some stories speak of embryos yet imperfectly formed or only half-human, incubating deep in the earth until the time is ripe for their emergence on the surface, there to enjoy what the creator has prepared for them. From the Iroquois comes a story of human beings living in darkness under the earth until one day, one of them found an opening and climbed out to the surface of the earth. As he walked along he saw a deer which he killed and took back down into the earth where his companions enjoyed the food. Since this was a good sign that the surface of the earth would provide them with a better life, they decided to emerge from the earth.[1]

In the Navajo language the earth is referred to as a recumbent Woman. There are four regions or worlds in the earth, called by the Zuni the four wombs. It was thought that in the beginning human beings lived in the deepest level and then gradually came to the surface through a lake or stream. In one myth Twins were born into the underground at the beginning of time. Coming through a lake they found people who took no solid nourishment but lived on the "steams and smells" of food. When the underground people saw the Twins eating solid food they were horrified because in the underground such food was thrown away. After many adventures the Twins led a number of people to the surface and from these, it was believed, humanity descended. This myth proposes a reason why the newly-born feed only on the "wind" until the moment when the "invisible cord" is cut. Then they can absorb milk and light nourishment, but only with difficulty.[2]

We see a connection here between the life in the pre-existence and the newborn babe. It is as if in the Zuni view every infant lived in its prenatal state in the deep earth. The Zuni creation story elaborates on this theme. Here the creator, feeling quite alone, transformed himself into the Sun and produced two seeds with which he impregnated the Great Waters. Then with his light shining on the waters, they grew to take the shape of Earth Mother and Father Heaven. From the union of Earth and Heaven many forms of life were born but Earth Mother kept them within her body, the "four wombs." From the deepest womb seeds germinated and then little by little forms of life began to crawl in the various layers. But one being distinguished by intelligence and in some manner "divine" appeared under the waters, and after emerging through all the four layers arrived on the surface of the earth. This being made his way to the Sun Father and begged him to rescue humanity and the creatures living within the earth. The Sun then repeats the impregnating process and Twins are again born. Here the Sun wishes to produce free and intelligent beings. The Twins are endowed with magical power and they go into the depths of the earth and make a ladder by which the humans and other creatures can ascend. This creation in Zuni tradition, as in all myths, happens in the center of the world, which, as Eliade points out, is "the Umbilical Matrix," or the Place of Gestation.[3]

Studies of Paleolithic and Neolithic Earth-Goddess civilizations portray the pregnant belly of the Earth Goddess from whom all life comes, for in these civilizations it was believed that the Mother created all things out of herself, including the sky and the rivers and all beings. All kinds of mounds have been found, including small ones such as loaves of bread and ovens symbolizing the goddess' pregnant belly. In all mythologies expressing the emergence of the embryo from the earth as creation, we find a repetition of the belief that return to the origins after separation and development, reactualizes on an archetypal level the renewing energies of creation.

Now let us turn to the alchemists. Who were they and what were they doing in their laboratories? How can their experiments and meditations be related to creation and rebirth? We can begin with the meaning of the word "alchemy." One meaning for the Arabic word *alkimia* is "black land or earth." Another meaning is "to fuse or cast a metal."[4]

Eliade suggested that the mythic background of alchemy is related to the ancient miners and metallurgists. The first myths and symbolism of miners, smelters and smiths, tell stories of Mother Earth incubating and bringing to birth with the help of the miners, the ores hidden in her "womb." He writes:

> Mineral substances, hidden in the womb of the Earth Mother shared in the sacredness attached to the goddess. Very early we are confronted with the idea that ores "grow" in the belly of the earth after the manner of the embryos. Metallurgy thus takes on the character of obstetrics. The miners and metal workers intern in the

unfolding of subterranean embryology. They accelerate
the rhythm of the growth of ores, they collaborate in the
work of Nature and assist it in giving birth more rapidly.[5]

In other words, human labor replaces time, perhaps thou-
sands of years, in the production of the "mature" metal.
This idea goes back to the second century B.C. to the Chinese
alchemists who believed that in the earth the "lesser" metals
became "greater," that the base minerals develop over thou-
sands of years into "noble" minerals, such as lead developing into gold. It was with the help of fire that the metal
workers transformed the ores, called "embryos" into mature
metal or gold. In this view gold was seen as the fruit of the
earth. The ores are not "common" but rather unripe or im-
mature. Nature has within itself the power to mature, to
perfect itself, to heal. This is the insight and the message of
alchemy.

It is not difficult to see why Jung was attracted to alchemy. With great enthusiasm he deciphered the difficult
alchemical texts, finding in them parallels to his own dis-
coveries of the psyche's healing powers. He resonated with
the alchemists' reverence for nature, a nature imbued with
spirit, almost in a mystical sense.

Although the alchemists were more or less aware that
their insights and truths were of divine origin, they knew
they were not sacred revelations but were vouchsafed by
individual inspiration or by the "lumen naturae," the
"sapientia Dei" hidden in nature.[6]

During the first centuries of the Christian era, perhaps due
to the rampant sensuality of the time and the need to focus
on cultural values, the feeling for nature as "godly" gave
way to the view of nature as dangerous. It was felt that

Christians could be led astray from the worship of the true God as Spirit if they contemplated nature as "spirit."

While earlier on it was thought that spirit unites all opposites and lives in everything, this idea gradually changed. While formerly spirit was personalized as Father and Earth as Mother; while matter was animated by spirits and demons who were considered divine; spirit later became associated with the intellect and matter came to be regarded as impersonal and "dead." As this happened we began to lose our emotional unconscious identity with nature and with that, we began to lose our contact with its symbolical quality. Today, "Thunder is no longer the voice of an angry god, nor is lightning his avenging missile. No river contains a spirit, no tree is the life principle of a man, no snake the embodiment of wisdom. . . ."[7] When nature is no longer the epiphany of the gods, then the unconscious compensates, for the repressed has retreated into psyche.

The alchemists stayed in tune with the mystery of matter. Within matter, they believed, lies hidden a god seeking redemption. Influenced by Gnosticism, which taught that at some time in the past a god as "breath" or animation had fallen and become imprisoned in matter, they saw themselves as "redeemers" or "saviors" of this imprisoned god. As Jung points out, the alchemists knew little about matter, and in the *opus,* as they watched the changes in the *materia* they had placed in the vessel, they projected their own unconscious into the process they watched. As for the "god" that was to be redeemed out of the earth, it was the "divine being" or the self within themselves, bound and wanting to be free, that they saw. The alchemist, then, as he worked and prayed in his laboratory sought to transform his own life.

As we begin now to look more closely at this alchemical *opus* let us keep in mind the central image. "This science," writes Jung, "is like a pregnancy, a mystery of becoming. It becomes out of itself through a development from dark to light."[8] The image of pregnancy as creation appears in various alchemical texts, and one Arabic text describes the fetus as a product of water, air, fire and earth. The fetus comes out of the earth. That is, psychologically "earth" refers to the human body and the birth takes place within the human personality, as change or transformation. This image of pregnancy is often present in alchemical writing describing the actual work in the laboratory.

The medieval alchemist's laboratory was a place of experiment, of prayer, and of philosophical reflection. In a round vessel representing the universe (or Earth Mother)

The alchemist, an hermetic philosopher. (Courtesy Picture Collection, New York Public Library.)

the alchemist placed a solution in which metals and substances were to be dissolved. These substances corresponded to "earth" and they remained at the bottom of the spherical-shaped vessel that had to be sealed to prevent leakage. Heat was applied, gently, at first, and the process began. As the "cooking" continued steam began to fill the upper half of the vessel and the contents began to undergo change. As we have seen, the alchemists sought to free from "matter" the soul or spirit they intuited was imprisoned there. Again we must remember that the alchemists knew little about the nature of matter or about their own subjectivity. This made it easier for them to project into the transformation of metals or earth their own desire for liberation. When we yearn within ourselves for completion and fullness of life we can easily project that lead wants to become gold, or that nature "groans" for completion.

From a psychological perspective Jung offered an analogy for the alchemical process. The darkness represents the collective unconscious, the deeper dimension of ourselves which, if it remains unknown, comes to be feared as "evil" or negative. Yet if we become conscious of this side of ourselves, we may discover that the unknown contains the highest value, i.e., the "gold," which is likened to an incorruptible healing power over melancholy and depression, and even over physical disease. For the alchemists, this value contained in the matter, this "stone" was called the new light, and alchemists believed that it had a life or spirit. This explains why they called it by human names, not only "child" but "our child" or "our son."

With patience, perseverance, with prayer and watching, the alchemists worked in their laboratory and their *opus* began to take on the appearance of a new creation. "The alchemists copied the process of creation in order to reach the original intention of the creator, and thus to find a means of transforming and enobling nature."[9] As with the creation myths the alchemists begin with the *prima materia,* the stuff or "chaos" out of which creation emerges, and as they watched the effect of fire on these metals and substances in the vessel, they named the developing process by stages or colors: the black or *nigredo,* the white or *albedo,* and the red, or *rubedo.* Each of these stages was associated with a metal. The metal of *nigredo* is lead; of *albedo,* silver; and of *rubedo,* gold. When we say that the alchemist identified with these stages, we mean that he was called to experience his own inner chaos, to suffer through his personal confusion and darkness and to name it or "contain" it as a necessary suffering with a meaning and a goal.

Nigredo is associated with lead, heaviness, and with depression, decay and death. We relate *nigredo* with the darkness of endings, such as we have seen at the winter solstice when the year or the cosmos was "wearing out" and the sun had disappeared. Psychologically, *nigredo* represents our own feelings of chaos, of being lost, abandoned, or of having fallen into a hole, not being able to find our way into a clearing. The darkness or blackness of *nigredo* may represent in our lives the dying out of certain attitudes or religious beliefs that served well for a time but are no longer useful and life-giving. Experiencing *nigredo* in our lives may feel like a death or a dying of the familiar and comfortable. Black is the color of the unconscious and the unknown. At such times we do not know what is going on in our lives. But it is important to remember that black also represents the good fertile earth, rich and nourishing, indeed, the source for the gestation and emergence of new life. Paradoxically, then, *nigredo* refers to hidden life and to the heaviness of lead as a kind of deadness. Jung quotes an alchemist who writes, "In the lead there is dead life . . ." a curious phrase.[10] This writer goes on to say that "dead life" is the great secret. Dead life is neither death nor life, but the boundary between the two, a mysterious thing, says Jung, who in his later writings talks about the gift or value hidden in the darkness of depression.

The second stage or color is associated with dawn. *Albedo* is related to the moon and to silver. The moon is the heavenly body of the night. Jung writes that gradually our personal situation may be lightened, as in a dark night the blackness is gradually illuminated by the rising moon. "This dawning light corresponds to the 'albedo,' the moonlight."[11] For the alchemist and for us, as well, the *nigredo* is the longest part of our inner journey. But the *albedo* comes after our period of suffering, as we begin to see the light. At first we experience a mixture of darkness and light; we do not see clearly, but the important thing is a lightening of spirit within us. We know that something has changed, even though our future path may not be clear.

The third stage, *rubedo,* corresponds to the metal, gold and to the planet, sun. In alchemy the *rubedo* corresponds to the joining of opposites, the sun and moon, into the new creation, the "child" or "the philosophers' stone." The following picture shows Mercurius as the divine child, psychologically reflecting the new attitude that comes out of the tension between the opposites. Mercurius is standing on the sun and moon, representing the conscious and unconscious. The birds indicate that the process is an inner, spiritual one, and the rays of the sun signify the heat or emotion necessary for the process.[12] Fire transforms the *prima materia,* the lead into gold. Red suggests blood, life, warmth, passion, inflammability, energy, love. The *rubedo* is the fruit of suffering. As we begin to more fully experience our own

The alchemical Mercurius as a "child," from the Mutus liber *(1677) by*
Altus. (Reprinted from The Golden Game *by Stanislas Klossowski de*
Rola, courtesy George Braziller, Inc.)

"red" as the potential and energy of the "divine child" we
are able to live more vitally, listening to our inner dreams,
and making decisions to achieve the vision of our own life.

If we image Advent as an inner *opus* we can perhaps
identify with the alchemist's quest. Remember that the medieval alchemists were, for the most part, practicing Cath-
olics who believed in Christ's incarnation and its saving
power. It was their desire to experience more personally this

salvation, or rather, to connect the dogma of incarnation to their own personal life. By meditating and experimenting in their laboratories, they came in touch with the transforming meaning of their own suffering. Whatever nuances our own inner journey takes on, it will no doubt parallel the color worlds of the alchemist: the black, the white, and the red, and the goal will be to recover an awareness and experience of our own value, and our worth as carriers of divinity. Symbolically Advent connects us to our roots in that divinity and thus to our present and to our dreams for our future.

Let us look briefly at some of the Advent motifs to be amplified more fully later. Because Advent repeats the process of creation it, too, begins in darkness. We become aware of this even in early November as nature itself prepares the way and the decay of autumn leaves enriches the earth. The sun hides its warming rays, and we are enveloped by darkness and cold. One season comes to an end. In the Advent imagery of the first week we note scenes of destruction and chaos. In one reading, Matthew 24:37f, cosmic floods come to destroy everything in the world except Noah and a few others who are saved in order to begin another "world." This "chaos" is pictured as death through water, psychologically, a return to the waters of the unconscious for rebirth. The first phase, then, of the dawn of a new creation in Advent, parallels the alchemist's *opus,* in which matter is broken up, regressing to its original chaos. Out of the chaos comes the possibility for renewal.

Another text read during the first week of Advent, Luke 21:21f, describes the apocalyptic events of destruction, not by water, but by fire. The powers of heaven are shaken, the earth destroyed by fire, and out of the ashes comes the new creation. Both texts, then, picture ending, death, the cosmic night. Personally they represent the end in us of what is worn out, stale, sterile, of no longer any use in our lives.

These images, too, may reflect the separation from the archetypal world so that we may be psychically "born" in our own right. This, too, feels like a "death." Of this aspect we shall see more later. Psychologically, it is here that we begin to experience the *nigredo,* the blackness and chaos, the first alchemical stage. We may feel at these times, as if nothing is moving in us, our energy is stuck and we feel isolated and "dead."

Following these images of destruction, the biblical Advent imagery focuses on John the Baptist who calls on his followers to prepare a way for the Lord. Paradoxically, the way toward the light leads further into the darkness of the wilderness. If we regard the wilderness as a place of sterility and death, which it truly is, we must, on the other hand admit that the wilderness is a place of transition and new life. The pattern repeats, something must die, an old way of being, to give way to the new. This is why we find the wilderness so threatening and fearful. Years ago I had an analysand who, in our first session together, said that he had been afraid to come because he feared I would destroy his personality. At first I had no idea what he meant. It soon became clear that by "his personality" he referred to his persona which had served him well but which he realized was now stifling something in him that wanted to live, his own emotional life. This man sensed that something in him needed to "die" if he would truly live.

In the wilderness we face the defenses that shield us from the "One" unrecognized in our midst, as the forces of darkness and light contend within us, our shadow forces. For those on the way to psychic birth or the discovery of the self, of "ground" within, the wilderness becomes the place where anger or rage become acceptable transforming powers, where we get in touch, perhaps for the first time, with our inner "fire." We can read the Baptist's exhortations to justice as a metaphor for the acceptance within ourselves of "the poor" and "rejected." Taken symbolically these rejected poor may represent our own feelings of poverty and worthlessness. Or perhaps in the wilderness we need to struggle with the demons of inflation and inferiority, our own emotional "highs" and "lows." Alchemically the wilderness represents the longest part of the process, the struggle with *nigredo* and its transformation through fire.

During the second and third weeks of Advent the liturgical texts offer images of baptism and descent into the river Jordan. The Baptist exhorts his followers to be baptized as a prerequisite for connecting with the "One" designated as Messiah. Psychologically this means that within the Advent context we begin to renew our relationship to God, or to the unconscious sources of life flowing within us. We begin to sense the good within, a hint, at least, of support and strength coming from a transcendent source. Already in this water symbolism there appears a glimpse of the *albedo*. The alchemist, staying with the process, was able to transform matter into a new form in which the "son" or "child" appears. So, psychologically, we begin to realize a sense of self and Self through concentration on our dreams and other unconscious processes. Gradually the *albedo* happens. As a symbol of transition to the New Kingdom, the Baptist images hope in the possibility of resurrection through suffering. Toward the end of the third week of the Advent liturgy the darkness and heaviness of "lead" begins its "silvering" process as dawn approaches. As the Baptist fades from the scene, moonlight and dew image the entrance into the fourth week of Advent with the text, "Drop down dew ye heavens. . . ."

The alchemists believed that within our own body, as within the earth, lie potential seeds of life that germinate through the life-giving water which they called dew or the

The Virgin as the "vas" of the divine child, from a 16th century Venetian painting.

sperm of life. The dew represented that healing elixir that falls from heaven or which, in the vessel or *vas,* appeared as the contents were heated. In ancient mythologies it is the Moon Goddess who is the giver of dew, the one who sends rain and who personifies fertility. The central alchemical image, the *vas* or the "round" in which the new creation takes place as the *rubedo,* represents the goddess. In Advent Mary represents the vessel. In the Catholic prayer, the Litany of Loretto, Mary is repeatedly referred to as *vas.* She is called, for example, the "vessel of honor," and "the vessel of devotion." As *vas* she carries within her the new creation, the "son," "child," "stone." As *vas* Mary is Mother who shares the attributes of Earth Mother as source and matrix of birth. As mirror and image of the sun she is called the Moon, the essence of *albedo.*

While the third stage of alchemy, the *rubedo,* belongs more appropriately to Christmas Day, its warmth and vitality are anticipated already at the annunciation where spirit and earth join and the "impossible" becomes possible. What happens at this moment is what the alchemist would consider the primeval revelation, or the secret found in the depth of every human being. That secret is the "gold" which lies within nature or, as Jung would say, within the human personality. For the alchemist the secret was revealed only to those who would agree to undergo the initiation, the descent into *nigredo.* This initiation consisted, for the alchemists, in certain "operations" performed on the matter within the vessel.

Four key operations leading to the *rubedo,* or the coming to earth, or incarnating of the "child," are related to the elements: water, air, earth and fire. The alchemists referred to the goal of their *opus* as a child begotten by the sun and moon, "cradled" by the four elements and nourished by the earth. One alchemist writes that the water preserves the fetus for three months and the fire preserves it for the same length of time. The air warms it for three months. While all the elements form the alchemical fetus, as Jung points out the fourth element is the earth and it is from here that the "child" comes.

How did the alchemists relate these abstract and cosmic texts to the actual work in the laboratory, and how can we relate them to ourselves as coming to "psychic birth"? The alchemists performed "operations" on the matter in their vessel in the laboratory, and four of these operations are directly related to the elements: *sublimatio, solutio, calcinatio* and *coagulatio. Sublimatio* refers to the vapor released as the contents burned in the alchemical vessel. Symbolically, *sublimatio* refers to the heavenly realm and to inspiration. *Sublimatio* elevates, being concerned with the "higher realms of spirit. While *sublimatio* can take us away from earthly existence if we are not grounded, making us "airy," "living in our head," it can give us a vehicle for living our creativity, as well as a connection with Spirit and the archetypal world. Another image for *sublimatio* is the ladder, reaching to the spirit world from earth to heaven. If symbolically we climb this ladder, we are initiated into the contemplation of the gods. Alchemists regarded birds as another image of *sublimatio,* the spirit world. It is well-known that in dreams birds often represent spiritual aspiration.

In contrast to sublimation, *solutio* is an operation in which the dry pieces of earth are dissolved in water, the return to a "chaotic" or mixed-up state, the *prima materia.* Water was also associated with a return to the womb for rebirth, and thus, in Christian symbolism, to baptism. The alchemists would dissolve substances, i.e., "earth" in their vessel, heat them and watch as vapors, referred to as "birds" or eagles ascended and then descended as condensed vapor.

This process fascinated them. The goal was to produce the most subtle of all spirit in the form of a fluid called "eternal water," a water likened to dew, which had fertilizing power. *Solutio* also refers to tears. When we are ungrounded, or longing to experience our real potential and our real self, we have a tendency to take solace in religion and the spiritual. But if this "flight" happens too early in life, we need to have our spiritual side "earthed." Crying helps us to release feelings of being "stuck" and unrelated to ourselves. Crying helps us to "come down" to earth. Returning to the waters of the womb (baptism) can be a healthy and life-saving movement. But surrender to a containment in the womb can be dangerous.

Calcinatio is the fire operation. Without fire nothing would happen in the alchemical vessel. Fire purifies and transforms. Fire is related to purification of instinctual animal energies as well as to those energies themselves. Fire is affect and emotion, sexuality and passion. As the fire operation is crucial to the "cooking" in the alchemical vessel, so fire or emotion is crucial to the therapeutic process. Without it nothing happens. On the way to psychic birth, fire relates both to the recovery of affect and to its purification. Experiencing our shadow fire as anger or rage deepens our sense of ego and leads us further along the way to *coagulatio*.

Coagulatio is the alchemical operation related to earth. Symbolically it is a process that "grounds" or turns something into earth. In the laboratory, for example, cooling can turn a liquid into a solid state, making the substance firm. Psychologically speaking, for a psychic content to become "earth" means that it has been concretized in a particular localized form; that is, it has become attached to an ego.[13] Acting to bring our desires and dreams into reality helps to incarnate or ground us, in alchemical terms, helps to

"coagulate" us. Getting in touch with our instinctive shadow energies adds fire to the process. If we become too "spiritual" without first experiencing our affect and our body,
there is a good possibility that we will feel disconnected
from our self and from others. The alchemists' description
of their "child" as born and nurtured from the elements
may seem to us abstract and unreal, yet this description
found its parallel in the operations performed in the laboratory on the *materia:* the dissolving operation as solution; the
firing of the contents as *calcinatio,* the purifying or vaporiz-
ing as *sublimatio* and the solidifying operation as *coagulatio.*
These operations were performed as needed in the process,
each contributing to the outcome, as new creation (see Jung
CW 12).

The alchemists relating their work to the elements
comes as no surprise to us if we recall that for centuries
astrology and Chinese medicine have worked with the relationship of body and psyche to the elements. In astrology
air signs (Gemini, Libra, Aquarius) are correlated with our
perception, and abstract thinking, fire signs (Leo, Aries,
Sagittarius) reveal our excitability and enthusiasm for self-
expression; water signs (Cancer, Scorpio, Pisces) symbolize
the feeling response, our capacity for empathy and our psychic sensitivity; and earth signs (Taurus, Virgo, Capricorn)
express our relation to the material world, our sense of
self-discipline and perseverance. Water and earth signs are
considered receptive, inward and containing; air and fire
signs as active and outward. For centuries the Chinese have
traced the patterns of the body landscape in its yin-yang
energies—dark, light, receptive, active energies. And present-
day Reichian and neo-Reichian theories postulate that
health comes through a balancing of energies within the
body. The fetal chart below shows the interweaving of air,
earth, fire and water in creating the basic energy relation-

ships in the body. Thus we note that our own body-psyche is deeply connected to the elemental energies, and our health is dependent on a harmonious relationship to them. Here we touch on the bodily dimension of the alchemical or symbolical child-god born from the earth and "nourished" by the elements.

A striking example of our longing for "at-one-ment" from a psychological perspective is recounted by Ann Ulanov of one of her analysands who suffered from anorexia nervosa. This woman confided a vision of the essential unity of reality, a coherence portrayed by the connectedness of the elements of life: earth, fire, air, water. In this woman's vision

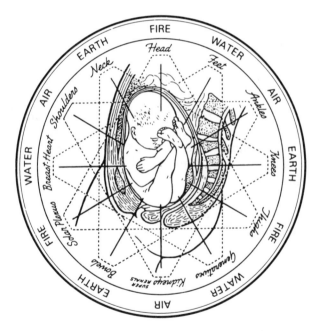

A fetal chart shows the interweaving of the four active elements to create the basic energy relationships of the human body.

she sees herself lying in the sun on a beach, "held in an encircling completeness of sand touching water and the water touching the sky."[14] Ulanov comments that all the elements surrounded and encompassed the woman's small reality and she felt "a liberation from complication and burden, able to deal with my problems because I am connected in my own body, just as the sky, earth, and water are connected around me."[15]

As we shall see, the Advent biblical texts can be viewed, in their general structure, after the pattern of the alchemical operations as liberating and bringing to birth what we long for as "at-one-ment" with ourselves and with God. During the first week of the Advent liturgy it is the solution or water operation that leads us first to destruction of the old (the Cosmic Flood) and back to beginnings. A new creation is about to take place. But the initiation leads us into the wilderness where during the second and third weeks we experience the fire of purification, and a renewal in water. During the fourth week air and earth symbolism dominate in the ascent/descent motif with the angel's greeting and the Child's conception. As the common theme in both alchemy and Advent is pregnancy and birth, so is the theme of uniting the opposites, of gathering and restoring into something new what has been separated. During Advent the theme of unity is represented by Christ, who as Son of Man gathers, judges, and redeems what was lost and scattered bringing them back into unity and wholeness:

> The Son of Man will send out the angels and gather His elect from the four winds, from the ends of the earth to the ends of heaven (Mk 13:24–27).

The vision of angels gathering from the four quarters of the earth recalls the alchemical initial "chaos" as undifferentiated and hostile elements in need, first, of separation, and then of reordering and gathering up. Psychologically this image offers an analogy to the work of Jungian analysis with its emphasis on looking at and experiencing our emotions and the different aspects of ourselves and "owning" them.

Restoration as an Advent theme is represented in the following text which gives assurance of recovery after the suffering of *nigredo* depression and fragmentation:

> Then moonlight will be bright as sunlight and sunlight itself be seven times brighter . . . like the light of seven days in one . . . on that day the Lord dresses the wound of his people and heals the bruises his blows have left (Isa 30:25–26).

Here the cosmos reflects the union of sun and moon and a new awareness as the rising of the sun. But the moon is described here as bright as the sun, a true "marriage" of opposites. Seven is a number of initiation, of stages or steps leading through transformative suffering to a healing that comes only from the recovery of what is truly oneself. This recovery is felt as an "at-one-ment" experience in which we begin to "see" the meaning of our suffering and fate as divinely given and purposeful. As in alchemy this "seeing" is an experience of our inner divine "spark," the goal of the Advent mystery.

In summary, we see that one of the underlying myths of Advent is the death-rebirth myth of alchemy. Alchemy is related to the creation myths which describe human "birth" from the earth. It became obvious to Jung that the alchemists' psychic suffering was projected into the *vas* or vessel where, through their experiments with matter, they witnessed and experienced their own death and rebirth. For the alchemists, nature is not separate from God, but rather unfolds and "lives" through men and women. The fruit of this unfolding is imaged at times as the child or the gold, the secret of immortality. It is also likened to the stone, which the builders rejected, a reference to Christ. At times the image is more personalized as "son." In their projections onto matter the alchemists experienced death and rebirth imaged as *nigredo, albedo,* and *rubedo,* and they intuited here as well the pattern of initiation as their need to experience and find meaning and purpose for their suffering. The "child" born through suffering comes from the "earth," from oneself, and is nourished by the elements. Each of us has our unique patterning of air, fire, water and earth and in our lifetime we experience analogously in our own "vessel" the alchemical operations.

The Advent imagery interweaves patterns of the elements, as it moves into *nigredo, albedo,* and *rubedo,* from darkness and chaos, to dawn and to rebirth. Finally, the alchemists longed for a sense of unity centered on the Elixir of Life, that gold or inner child of promise. And is not this, too, the goal of our own Advent longing?

3

Hope

Hope is synonymous with Advent, the season that celebrates the approach of the divine child. When hope is alive in us we can envision the future, for the future already stirs within us. Hope is an aspect of our longing and is born out of our loneliness. It would seem that there in the depths of our despair hope awakens, often imaged as "child." Let us now reflect on the themes of loneliness and hope in some of the religious and psychological contexts as they weave around the image of child: the "dream" child, the real child, the mythological child-god, and the divine child. All of these aspects of "child" resonate in our experience of Advent hope.

We may think that hope is primarily an adult virtue. But psychologist Heinz Kohut writes with amazement at how children cope with loneliness and loss. Children who were subject to a variety of seductions, to beating, to manipulations, to unbearable intrusiveness—together with something more detrimental to self-development, the cold, grim atmosphere in which they grew up—do manage to survive. "How," asks Kohut, "do these children become reasonable well-functioning and clearly non-psychotic adults?" Kohut answers, ". . . they never quite gave up hope."[1]

What is this hope? From a psychoanalytical perspective hope is a drive that wars against fragmentation and destruction. Hope is related to the life instinct. Karl Menninger spoke of hope as the "mysterious working of the repetition compulsion, the very essence of which is a kind of relentless and indefatigable pursuit of resolution and freedom."[2] From the viewpoint of analytical psychology, it would seem that hope is related to the transcendent function, the symbol-making capacity of psyche that works to keep conscious and unconscious in dialogue. In this sense hope helps us to cope with loss and it moves us forward. In the Greek myth, Pandora releases the evils from her box, but hope remains on the bottom, perhaps a sign that we must reach bottom and take back our own evils, or shadow qualities, in order to stimulate hope. As we adults begin to integrate some of our shadow, we can begin consciously to experience emotions repressed in childhood.

The Hebrew word for hope means "to wait," an often repeated Advent motif. The same root *Qwh* is the base of a Hebrew word *tigwah* meaning "cord" or "rope."[3] "Hope is a rope," writes Angelus Silesius.[4] It is a rope anchored in the sky. Eliade elaborates on the ancient motif of ascension and the mythic rope joining earth to heaven at the cosmic center of the world. The rope or thread also connects conscious to unconscious, eternity to history. On the rope the shaman climbs to the other world to recover the lost soul. "To the observer," writes Desroche, "it seems that there is nothing to keep (the rope) up, except for the impalpable and inconsistent world of fantasy . . . and yet this rope is anchored. *It holds.* And when humans grab hold of it and pull themselves up, it takes the strain. . . ."[5] In contrast to the image of hope "anchored" in the sky, is hope in Christian symbolism pictured as a woman, sometimes with wings, arms raised to heaven, an anchor at her feet. While hope uplifts and frees, it does so only when anchored in the deep, as the anchor, thrown into the deep, steadies the ship. Biblically, hope is activated only through suffering, when we have reached rock bottom. Then true hope appears, in contrast to grandiose false hope, anchoring the soul so that it can endure affliction (Hebrews 6:18).

The French writer Charles Péguy offers another image of hope as a "pull" into the future. It is a poignant image of hope—a little girl who goes off to school walking between her two older sisters, Love and Faith. Looking at the three sisters, passers-by think that little Hope is being led by the other two, each of whose hand she holds. But a closer look reveals that the younger is pulling forward the two older girls.[6] In Péguy's view hope is superior to either faith or love. During the Advent-Christmas season this image recalls another image from Isaiah in which a child leads us out of conflict and chaos into a new and promising future.

The child is an image of hope, and as every therapist knows, it is not unusual at the beginning of therapy for a woman to express the wish to have a baby. Behind this wish may be the longing to be "born" into her real life, to experience her own self. In the lives of two women who were my analysands, we see how this desire for a child manifests itself in different ways. These women agreed to share some of their material and what follows are two brief composites with names and certain details changed to preserve anonymity.

Sylvia was twenty-three, an intelligent attractive woman who had suffered from bouts of depression and had attempted suicide during her late teens. She remembered her mother as hardworking, "trying to cope with me and my three sisters." Her father she feared. She remembered his shouting angrily at the slightest provocation, either taunting

her, or, at times, simply ignoring her. Sylvia longed for closeness and affection. When, as a child, she would hold on to
visitors or would climb on to their laps, her mother would
reprimand her. As she grew older Sylvia excelled in school,
always finding herself in classes for the intellectually gifted.
Yet her excellent academic record failed to bring her the
attention and affection she craved.

During the first few weeks of therapy Sylvia spoke of
her longing to have a baby. She felt depressed because
another short-lived relationship had ended, one of many.
Sylvia again felt like a "no-body." Later, while out for a
weekend with some friends, Sylvia said she "overdid the
drinking and the sex part, but I don't care. I hope I got pregnant." And not many weeks later, she told me that, indeed,
she was.

During the next few months Sylvia and I met every
week. She began fantasizing about the baby and doing
some realistic planning centering around its care and support. She began feeling like "somebody" and continued to
gain insight into her own life story. Two months before the
baby was due, she returned to her home in another city
where her parents welcomed her. Some time later, I received
a picture of her cradling in her arms a baby girl. The road
ahead would be difficult, she knew, but she felt "into" her
life, and she would travel the road.

In contrast to Sylvia, Melanie was a twenty-seven-year-
old married woman. Early in therapy she, like Sylvia, announced that she wanted to have a baby. Earlier in their
marriage she and her husband had decided to delay having
a family until they were more settled in their professions.
But, it seemed to Melanie, the time had come. She had been
thinking about it for some time but still hesitated to discuss
it with her husband. She could not explain her ambivalent

feelings about bringing up the subject. Melanie described her childhood as happy. Her father, a kindly shy man whom she felt she never really knew, readily deferred to her mother, an outgoing expressive woman who took great pride in her children. Above all this family valued peace and harmony, and it was unheard of to express anger or any other so-called negative emotion. Gradually Melanie began to realize the extent to which she had repressed her own spontaneity.

Melanie had never done dream work before and it opened for her another world, gradually putting her in dialogue with "unborn" aspects of herself. Her initial dream pointed in a striking way to her psychic situation. During our third session together, she told me this dream:

> There was a market with booths. Some women were there. It looked like a Christmas bazaar but it wasn't Christmas. I looked around at some ornaments. But I had to go to the bathroom. The toilets are strange in form and the floor is covered with water. I think it is overflowing. It seems to be in an airport waiting room. I don't seem to be able to go to the bathroom.

To the word "bazaar" Melanie associated "wandering around and buying trinkets." Could the dream suggest that the dreamer is being called to experience her wholeness, that is, to find the personal meaning of Christmas for her, but that she is caught in a "wandering" kind of life looking at "trinkets?" On one level this would not seem to be true since Melanie takes her professional life seriously and is a competent and caring social worker.

But perhaps the dream points to another kind of "wandering." Urination in dreams often symbolizes the dreamer's affirming and expressing his or her personal uniqueness.

Clogged up or overflowing toilets point to enormous repression of emotion and spontaneity, unintegrated aspects of the shadow. Toilets in exposed public places may point to a lack of frame or inner container in the dreamer where she can "be" or feel "good" about herself by "letting go." This dream brought up something that Melanie hesitated to admit: her pattern of deferring to her husband. She had often felt "put down" by her husband if she made choices not to his liking: a new dress, sporting equipment, etc. But she found it difficult to say anything to him. She "swallowed" her feelings.

A month later Melanie dreamed:

> I'm pregnant and the baby is a small rubber and metal contraption with hooks or claws like a lobster. It has clear plastic over the tips of metal on the claws. The head is very mechanical looking like the inside of a watch . . . I thought it was okay. The "baby" was attached to my ear.

Showing me a picture she had painted, Melanie said that she could not find a red paint red enough to paint the "baby's" body. The head she had done with intricate detail in black and white. She remembered that in the dream the body was tightly covered with plastic. The head, like the inside of a watch, reminded her of herself. "I live in my head, always planning, organizing, doing." In the picture the red representing blood, life, emotion, sexuality, contrasts sharply with the black and white of the head. Perhaps what is "kept in" tightly enclosed and wrapped in plastic, is the fire which would add vibrancy and vitality to her personality.

This dream image appears at first weird and non-human, and this is true of many images that come up at the beginning of the psychic process. They appear chaotic and strange and unacceptable. Much later Melanie and I began to see more clearly how this image shows her basic pattern and indicates her way to wholeness in the recovery of her "red," her repressed emotion and spontaneity. "Isn't it odd," Melanie said, "that this dream 'baby' is attached to my ear?" "Perhaps," I responded, "this means that you need to listen to your heart." The ear is associated with the spiral and shell, both feminine images; the shell is a birth symbol related to the vulva. In a Chinese diagram for the study of acupuncture, the ear is pictured as an inverted fetus. It was said that Karma, the son of the sun god Surya, was born from his mother's ear, and sometimes in Christian tradition the Spirit as a dove impregnates the Virgin by entering her ear.[7] The ear, then, hears the creative word and listening to the word (the meaning of the word "obedience" is "to listen"), brings forth new life.

The wish to have a baby often expressed by women during the first weeks of analysis may be interpreted in some cases as a desire to experience more fully a sense of self. It may be that Sylvia's need led to physical pregnancy as well as to a greater insight into her history and her need for parenting. In contrast, Melanie began to discover through her dreams her inner child's need to be "heard" in expressing its dreams, desires, and needs. It is in this area that both women came more fully in touch with their loneliness and their longing.

In our society we do not like to talk about our loneliness. We talk about creative solitude, our need to do "creative" work. We are less likely to say "I am lonely." We find it easier to refer to the socially "deprived" and their loneliness: the homeless, those confined in prison, or the elderly isolated in tenement houses. Often it is "they" who are lonely. Psychologists speak of the loneliness experienced by borderline or narcissistic personalities. But, to some degree, it is we, each of us who is lonely. Psychologist Robert Hobson distinguishes between two kinds of loneliness, which he calls "cut-offness" and "no-being."[8] Both modes are related to our experience of love and loss. In "cut-offness" we have our thoughts and a rich fantasy world but we feel isolated and unable to communicate our inner wealth. It may be that we have been taught as children that the way we really feel is not our real self and thus not "good." Such children as adults often dream of glass houses or of being enclosed in a room with many windows. Years ago a woman I knew summed up in one image the atmosphere of her childhood. "I was sitting alone looking out the window. It seems I did that often." Only as an adult did she realize how lonely and "cut-off" she had felt. For while we can see through glass, there is no touching or warm feeling contact possible. If we feel "cut-off" we may appear to others as aloof and independent, not needing others. Behind this facade we hide our longing for warmth and intimacy. In "cut-offness" we have not experienced—at least, not enough—acceptance and love just for being ourselves.

Hobson's phrase "no-being" also refers to early experiences of love and separation. If from the beginning of our life we have a strong experience of being loved, it is easier to begin to internalize that realization even when we are separated from our loved ones. We "carry" the loved one with us. But when our sense of security is tenuous, we need others to be there present for us. We do not experience a basic trust in ourselves, so that in separation we may feel abandoned, and our terror can border on a sense of being annihilated. In our isolation we feel "no-being," alienated even from our own body. Nobody is there. A young woman explained to me that when she left her family to go on a trip, something she avoided as much as possible, she relived a scene from childhood. In this scene she was in a field of boulders crying and screaming for someone to come. Running from one boulder to another, she experienced the isolation of neither being able to be seen nor heard. Later on in life, separation brought on feelings not only of isolation, but of abandonment and "no-being," feeling of being "no one."

Most of us feel neither of these extremes of "cut-offness" or "no-being." Yet at certain times in our life we may find ourselves falling into confusion and chaos. C. G. Jung faced his own "cut-offness" during five years between 1913 and 1918 when he tried to bridge his inner and outer world, "hoping that from the psychic depths which cast up the powers of destruction the rescuing forces will also come."

> The consequence of my resolve, and my involvement with things which neither I nor anyone else could understand, was an extreme loneliness. I was going about laden with thoughts of which I could speak to no one: they would only have been misunderstood. I felt the gulf between the external world and the interior world of images, in its most painful form. I could not yet see that interaction of both worlds which I now understand.[9]

Jung goes on to say that he saw only irreconcilable contradiction between the "inner" and "outer" worlds. To make contact with the outer world and with people he had to succeed in showing that the contents of psychic experience are real. Otherwise, "I would be condemned to absolute isolation."[10] Jung found that when he could translate the emotions he experienced during this time into images, then he felt peaceful and reassured, "at-one" with himself. This language of images served to bridge inner and outer. They carried universal instinctual energies, "the real but invisible roots of consciousness."[11] These energies he personified as Self, Shadow, Animus, Anima, Mother, Father, Hero and Child.

Indeed, it is an "act of grace" for us when we experience an inner image or dream figure as real. When this happens the psychic energy in us that has been blocked can flow again bringing with it an opening of the prison door enabling us to take a new direction in life. Jung wrote extensively on the image of child as a carrier of energy, especially when we feel a loss of soul and the need for renewal. Because we can project our need for savior or redeemer, we see that in many myths this projection takes the form of a child-god. In mythology the child-god often is an orphan, having lost or never having had a mother. In Italian myth the child Tages sprang out of the earth, a child of Mother Earth.[12] The Greek god Dionysus was born after his mother's death. Other stories recount the emotional or physical abandonment of the child-god, who then becomes a solitary who is at home in the psychic or primeval world.[13] Frequently the child-god is warmed and fed by animals. Romulus and Remus were suckled by a she-wolf. Often in fairy tales the jealous king or others seek to destroy the child, but in spite of these threats, the child-god is invincible, escaping by supernatural means and overcoming as a hero those who would destroy it. It is as if the child-god's solitude strengthens him and puts him in touch with miraculous powers.

It would seem that children, especially children who suffer physical or emotional abandonment and are paralyzed by fear, are in touch with the archetype of the child-god in a special way. Having been "used" in some way these children protect themselves in miraculous ways, forming a body that both defends and expresses their story. Often their weakened ego fantasizes itself as superior, independent, powerful, not needing anyone, able to do everything alone. But alongside this self-image exists the poor, weak, vulnerable side. Somewhere between the "highs" and "lows" lies a cavern of loneliness and emptiness. And herein lives the child-god offering the strength of hope.

In the emptiness of loneliness and depression suffered by many children and adults hope "hides," as it were, like a seed dormant beneath the frozen landscape. Hope bides its time waiting for the ice to melt and the soil to warm. As one woman expressed it, "I knew something was very wrong in my family, but I consoled myself that it couldn't go on like this forever . . . someday I would be free." Psychologically when we experience an impasse within in our conscious life, when our energy is stuck, or one of our psychic functions is worn out, something is stirred up on an archetypal level to come to our aid, a manifestation from the unconscious, the inner Wisdom or Self. The child image often carries this new energy.

In Jung's view this is what happened historically in the period before the birth of Christ. At that time the religions of Greece and Rome had grown sterile. The symbols and the gods failed to mean anything in people's lives. They longed for a new age, for a savior. The poet Vergil expressed this longing for a new age the image of a child:

> Now a new generation comes down from
> high heaven. Only do thou, chaste
> Lucina, favor the birth of the child,
> through whom the iron brood shall cease
> to be, and a golden race arise
> throughout the world . . .[14]

Later Christian writers saw here a prophecy of the Christ Child who would usher in the new period of freedom. Jung saw the years preceding the birth of Christ as a time of darkness when with a sense of urgency the archetypal energy imaged as child or *Anthropos* (humanity) stirred in the collective unconscious. In Jung's view this image expresses the affinity between the God-man and the hope stirring within the unconscious of every man, woman and child to become integral and whole.

This powerful inner disposition of the psyche toward wholeness was symbolized by the Christ figure:

> Christ would never have made the impression he did on his followers if he had not expressed something that was alive and at work in their unconscious. Christianity itself would never have spread through the pagan world with such astonishing rapidity had its idea not found an analogous psychic readiness to receive them.[15]

In Jung's view the psyche contains in itself a potentiality for relation to God. "As the eye is to the sun so the soul corresponds to God."[16] The longing within each of us is to live as responsibly committed and surrendered to the *Imago Dei* as the historical Jesus expressed this in his union with the Father.

During Advent our hope and longing for a savior reach their most intense expression in the "O" Antiphons. During the Middle Ages these antiphons were sung from December 17th to 23rd during the solemnity of vespers in cathedrals and monasteries all over Europe. Today they continue to be recited or sung during the fourth week of Advent. Whether we have forgotten them or have never heard them, the spirit of their song dwells within us in our own longing for the Christ whom Jung sees both as the historical redeemer and as a symbol of the Self. From a psychological viewpoint the goal of our life is a conscious relation to the Self, the center of unity and the center of our fullest potential. "The Self is not only the center, but also the whole circumference which embraces conscious and unconscious."[17] The Self is an ordering principle and guide within and "around" us. In religious terms this concept comes closest to being expressed in St. Paul's words, "In Him we live and move and have our being," and again, in the words, "I live now, not I, but Christ lives in me." The Self is a God-Image comparable, in Jung's view, to the alchemists' "stone" symbol symbolizing that indestructible or immortal inner ground of our being.

Viewing the "O" Antiphons subjectively we may see them as expressions of longing for a closer relation to the Self or to God. Christ is addressed as Wisdom, King, Dawn, etc., all archetypal images representing powerful inner energies. In some ways the progression of images in the seven antiphons may be viewed as parallels to the alchemical or to any initiatory process which begins with the *prima materia,* often referred to as Wisdom, and is completed with the awareness of the "stone" or "child," Emmanuel, or "God within us." Let us look now at these beautiful antiphons of hope in the coming possibility of salvation and rebirth. The first antiphon pleads for Wisdom to show the way:

> O Wisdom, O holy word of God, you govern all creation with your strong yet tender care. Come and show your people the way to salvation.

While Wisdom appears in the Bible as Sophia (Wisdom 7:25, Sirach 24:3), it seems that the dominant image of Wisdom in Christianity has been the masculine Logos, the Word, the creative Son of God in whom all forms and ideas reside eternally. Psychologically, Wisdom is feminine. As the *Sapientia Dei,* Wisdom is the name given to the feminine

side of the unconscious. She holds the seeds of life hidden
in our unlived or neglected life, those aspects of our life still
waiting to be "incarnated." In alchemy, Wisdom is one name
given to the alchemical *prima materia,* that primal "stuff" or
chaos from which everything is born. The alchemists called
it Sapientia, or Sophia. "Everything is born from Sophia,"
as from the Earth Mother.[18] The most important task in life
was to experience this wisdom as a source of possibilities.

In the second antiphon God is addressed as the Lord of
Israel:

> O Sacred Lord of ancient Israel who showed yourself to
> Moses in the Burning Bush, who gave him the holy law
> on Sinai mountain, come, stretch out your mighty hand
> to set us free.

Fire is a manifestation of God. As eternal fire God appears
in the burning bush as later the Spirit would appear at Pen-
tecost as tongues of fire. Fire transforms. The alchemical
action of fire, *calcinatio,* hastens the process whereby the
nigredo and darkness turn into light. Fire is psychic energy,
inexhaustible and renewable. We feel alive when we express
emotion, when we live in tune with our heart's desire. In
depression our fire is pressed down, unfelt, unreachable.
We feel cold and isolated. We need a power within to release
the fire.

In the third antiphon the key image, Flower, relates us
to feeling and emotion.

> O Flower of Jesse's stem, you have been raised up as a
> sign for all peoples; kings stand silent in your presence;
> the nations bow down in worship before you. Come, let
> nothing keep you from coming to our aid.

Symbolically, a child rising from a flower suggests the birth of a god or a new beginning. The Christ Child is imaged as a rose blooming in the night. Divinities are said to have emerged from a flower. The Buddha, for example, is said to have emerged from the lotus as a matrix or womb.[19] Flowers are also associated with Paradise and birth. In this antiphon, Christ is called the flower of Jesse's stem. Jesse was David's father. Christ comes from David's line. The flower symbolizes feeling and the feminine from which flows life, expanding into new possibilities.

We have already referred to the next antiphon in the introduction but let us repeat it here:

> O Key of David, O royal Power of Israel, controlling at your will the gate of heaven. Come, break down the prison walls of death for those who dwell in darkness and the shadow of death; and lead your captive people into freedom.

The key symbolizes power. Christ is invoked here as the one who has power to open and close, to bind and to loose, to imprison or to free. In myth the keeper of the keys is the god, Janus, after whom January is named. He is the keeper of the keys who opens the future, the new year, and closes the old. As god of the old and new he looks backward and forward. As holder of the keys, Janus is connected with New Year symbolism and the rebirth of time. It is appropriate during Advent that Christ is invoked as key, the One who has power to open and to free. In alchemy the goal is sometimes called key as the Egyptian *ankh* symbolizing immortality.

We can sense the imagery in the fifth antiphon moving us closer to the goal of Advent:

> O Radiant Dawn, splendor of eternal light, sun of justice, come, shine on those who dwell in darkness and the shadow of death.

Dawn is the transition between the end of night and the beginning of day. The alchemists call dawn the "Mother of the sun."[20] As *albedo* the dawn signifies illumination and hope. Psychologically, dawn images growing consciousness. In this antiphon Christ is addressed as Dawn, as the beginning of a new day whose sun will shine on those who are frozen and near death. As "Sun of Justice" Christ will address injustice and will restore peace. The theme of justice is an important one in Advent where Christ is described as coming to us in a "cloud" of justice to redress wrongs. Basically, justice means giving to others what is due to them. Kierkegaard noted that the world pays little attention to those who suffer the loss of a self, less than if one had lost a leg or an arm or a large sum of money. To bring justice means to weigh or judge, that is, to separate false from true value and to restore what is true. If we view Advent as an image of longing for our own truth and life represented in Christ, then Christ as dawn and sun of justice symbolize what we need for survival: a deeper experience of our own fire, our self.

In the sixth antiphon, Christ is called on as king and sun.

> O King of all nations, the only joy of every human heart,
> O Keystone of the mighty arch of humanity, come and save the creature you have fashioned from the dust.

King and keystone are two images expressing unity. In discussing the cosmogonic myth and the Saturnalia festivals we saw that the king represents the new sun, the restoration of fertility and of possibility of ongoing life. In times past it was thought that when the king lives as the center of the nation he gives "soul" and vitality to the people. Christ as king represents the cosmic point of connection uniting heaven, earth, and the underworld. He is the Center of Creation unifying all. In this antiphon Christ is addressed as Keystone. A keystone is a wedge-shaped piece at the crown of an arch that holds the other pieces in place. The keystone, then, is the support of all. The reference suggests a passage in Ephesians 2:14: "He is the peace between us, and has made the two into one and broken down the barrier which used to keep them apart. . . ."

> O Emmanuel, king and lawgiver, desire of all the nations, Savior of all people, come to set us free, Lord our God.

As in the first antiphon Christ is addressed as Wisdom, that from which all new forms arise, the seventh and last antiphon evokes him as Emmanuel, the "God with us," "God within us." Alchemically, Wisdom is *prima materia,* the beginning of creation, Emmanuel is the goal, the child or stone. While we commemorate during Advent the historical birth of Jesus, it is the longing for an inner "birth" that we invoke in Emmanuel, or, rather, Emmanuel *is* the image of the birth of God in the soul. Psychologically this birth represents a growing awareness of who we are, where we have come from and where we are going.

For years these "O" Antiphons have epitomized the religious expression of longing for the messiah. They have been a source of comfort and hope in the messiah's coming. Today the imagery still speaks to us of our existential longing, not for a God from without who comes to save us, but as a call to the God within us. It would seem as if longing has been placed in us to draw us back again to our roots. And often loneliness is our way toward discovering the Messiah or saving power within us.

We have seen that longing is often expressed in therapy as a wish for a child, and the child image appears frequently in the dreams of both men and women as an image of a "young" aspect of ourselves, a potential to be developed. Psychologist Robert Hobson describes two poles of isolation experienced by many people today. One pole is the feeling of being cut off from ourselves and others. When this happens we tend to hide our own loneliness under a persona of well-being and independence. The other pole is the feeling of "no-being" or emptiness. During Jung's creative struggle with a sense of isolation, he discovered images to express and contain his emotion. His dialogue with the unconscious led him from a sense of "imprisonment" into freedom. Whatever our own feelings of "cut-offness" or isolation, it is within our longing that hope "hides" like a seed dormant beneath the frozen landscape. Hope bides its time waiting for the ice to melt, waiting for the soil to soften. It is the Advent message that speaks of this warmth and hope, of the inevitability of the sun's coming. The refrain of the "O" Antiphons, "Come, set us free," is the plea from the depths of our loneliness, not only a plea for the birth of God but for our own birth, or rebirth.

We approach now the first week of the Advent liturgy which brings us back to the beginnings: to darkness, chaos and destruction and, as well, to an awakening of hope. We are preparing for psychic birth. During the first week of Advent it is as if we are awakened from the sleep of unconsciousness and into the *nigredo* of the alchemists. At the same time we are awakened to hope in ourselves and in the God already dwelling within us.

4

Fear

In Christianity the death-rebirth pattern of initiation is more readily associated with Lent and Easter than with Advent and Christmas. Easter celebrates victory over death; Advent prepares for birth. Darkness and light, suffering and joy are linked in both. Both result in an awakening to a new level of consciousness, and such awakening can stir up our fear. It is our fear of change that causes us to fear unknown parts of ourselves. Our unconscious fear of the unknown seems to caution even against our own growth into psychic birth. On the one hand we yearn for it, on the other, there is a side of us that prefers to "sleep." The biblical texts of the First Sunday of Advent can be viewed as a drama of this psychological conflict. Let us look now at these motifs of sleep and awakening, of destruction and separation. These themes appear against the background of two images: the mountain and the Son of man. Relating to these ancient mythic patterns we will look at some psychological aspects of separating and "birth," and we will look, too, at aspects of an analytical "initiation" in which a thirty-five-year-old man faces his fear and begins to "awaken" to the reality and importance of his everyday world.

With the ancient texts we begin where all creation begins, at the Center of the Earth, the *axis mundi* where awakening is linked with the image of the mountain. In one of the first readings of the Advent liturgy all the nations of the world are pictured streaming to the mountain of Zion:

> In the days to come
> the mountain of the Temple of the Lord
> shall tower above the mountains
> and be lifted higher than the hills.
> All nations will stream to it,
> peoples without number will come to it; and they
> will say:
>
> "Come, let us go up to the mountain of the Lord,
> to the Temple of the God of Jacob
> that he may teach us his ways
> so that we may walk in his paths; . . ."
>
> (Isaiah 2:2–3)

Like the image of the cosmic tree or ladder, the mountain represents that point where heaven, earth and the underworld meet and where it is easier to move between these realms. This explains why we refer to it as a place of change or transformation.

Mountains are associated with fertility and vegetation, and Mount Zion's height was linked to the location of Paradise from which the four living rivers flowed. The Hebrew scriptures picture Paradise as an enclosed garden, a circle of security and containment, the Garden of Eden. Eventually temples replaced the image of Paradise. Mountain heights came to represent the high realms of Spirit and the abode of the gods. As the highest place in the world the Cosmic mountain was a refuge from disaster, a place of shelter and protection. In both biblical and mythological tradition mountain imagery is linked to spirit and to nature.

This is apparent from the fact that while the summit of the mountain is the place nearest the gods, the mountain is also the navel, the place where creation begins. It was said that the world was created beginning at Zion and then spread out in different directions. There is an ancient tradition that pictures Adam as created in the Center of the earth, and redeemed at the spot where Jesus was later crucified at Golgotha. For the alchemists, mountains represented the *prima materia;* the matrix of inner possibility; the "inside" of the mountain contains the seed, or the fetus. Thus mountains serve as protecting vessels (*Sich bergen* means "to take refuge"; *sich verbergen* means "to hide."[1]) The alchemists refer to the inner mountain as the uterus or philosopher's oven, where the work of heating, incubation, and transformation proceed. For them the temple is not at the top, but within the *Hohle* or "cave." Here is the place of rebirth. It was believed in the ancient Near East that while the mountain was the scene of creation, it also contained energy and vital forces within to regenerate the dead. Thus the dead were returned here in order to be reborn. The mountain represents death, life, endings, and beginnings. It is a "union of opposites" or *coniunctio.*

In Christian mysticism, ascending the mountain has always been related to the quest for self-knowledge. Symbolically the Advent journey is that quest, the knowledge and the treasure sought personified by the child. That the mountain is associated with Paradise allows us perhaps to digress at this point to consider in more detail the meaning of Paradise as it relates to our own psychic birth and continuing "incarnation." Psychologically, Paradise can represent a desire to be sheltered from the world of conflict and struggle, the world where incarnation happens. Mario Jacoby writes that longing for Paradise means longing for "home" in those who do not feel "at home" in themselves.

This is a kind of "homesickness" for Paradise, and this longing is probably not directed at the personal mother, "but rather at a mother of the inner world who does not exist and perhaps never did exist in external reality. This, at bottom, is longing for one's own well-being. . . ."[2] Jacoby distinguishes between a longing for a past Paradise and the quest for the future Paradise symbolized by the kingdom of God. The one longing can be regressive and preventive of "incarnation"; the other is a goal to attain, through our personal initiation.

Child psychologists talk about the infant and its early development as a gradual psychic separation from the mother. At first, infant and mother are "one," and the infant experiences a sense of power, of omnipotence stemming from the fact that when he or she is hungry, food appears! If the infant is wet or otherwise uncomfortable it soon begins to feel better, as if by "magic." No sooner does the infant wish, than the wish is fulfilled. Because the infant does not sense itself as separate from the mother, it feels as if it has power to bring about these comforts. This sense of power needs to be fostered, that is, this fantasy of total bliss, "Paradise." But as the child develops, he or she begins to know, "I am not that powerful but I love and am loved by my parents and they are powerful. They will help me." In this experience of that "I am powerful with the strength of one who loves me," the child grows into a joyful experience of itself. One result of failure in this experience of power happens if the infant's need for food, holding, and support are not met. Then he or she feels frustrated and angry, helpless and inadequate.

Already at this stage the infant may begin to comply with others' expectations, repressing its own rhythms and spontaneous needs. We have referred to the Iroquois creation myth in which human beings lived under the earth until one day one of them came out into the light, found a deer, and took it back underground to feed the others who, on discovery that the earth provided such good things, decided to emerge. To use this analogy with the infant who comes into the world from the blissful womb of Paradise, we can say that if the earth does not seem to provide good things, the infant retreats back into Paradise to get its real needs met, and begins to meet the world with a "false self," hiding its true instinctual responses and needs, because it knows that these will not be accepted. The child's incarnational pattern is blocked. He or she has one foot in the archetypal world.

Such children grow into adulthood looking up to the sky, or to the spirit world, or to far-away places where they can find the peace they long for. They can live in a fantasy world of their own greatness, while feeling deeply insecure. Their approach to life includes a "BUT." I would take that job, "but." I think I love that woman, "but." The present situation never seems quite right. Real life will happen later, in the future. There is fear of committing oneself to the present. This fear reminds us of the baby's fear to "emerge" from "Paradise" if it senses that the environment is unwelcoming. It is important for such people, if they are not to retreat into the "sleep" of a regressive Paradise, to find an emotional connection with the images that bring peace and connectedness and, in doing so, to awaken to their personal power and their uniquely purposeful life. We shall return to the image of the mountain, but now it may be helpful for us to imagine what it is in our own life that we need to awaken *from* or what we need to awaken *to*.

Advent begins with a stirring call to "Awake!"

> You must wake up now . . . Our salvation is near . . . the
> night is almost over, it will be daylight soon (Romans
> 13:11–14).

What is this sleep that we so urgently are called to awaken
from? Is it the sleep of death, of forgetting, of ignorance? In
Greek mythology sleep and death are twin brothers, Hypnos
and Thanatos. So, too, Christians and Jews elaborated on
the relation between sleep and death (Job 3:13–15, Ecclesi-
astes 9:3). Awakening can mean "sobering up," coming to
our senses while staying asleep may indicate a desire to re-
main unconscious. Traditionally, overcoming sleep is part
of the ordeal of initiation where the novice is required to
stay awake through the night, or even for two or three con-
secutive days and nights.

   It is true that sleep can represent a call from the unconscious to listen to its voice in dreams. But sleep may indicate
our refusal to wake up. At times our sleep may resemble
that of Jonah who, upon receiving a message from God to
preach at Ninevah, said in so many words, "I can't do it, not
that! I'm not capable." Jonah then regressed into "sleep"
and, swallowed by a whale, moved through another initiation and into a new level of consciousness. Sleep can also
indicate fear and hopelessness. Psychologically the ego has
a tendency to regress when confronted with a decisive or
momentous event. For example, often in fairy tales at a
climactic point the hero or heroine falls asleep. When faced
with powerful psychic values that require watchfulness,
courage and perseverance, we find it almost impossible to
stay awake. When Jesus exhorted the disciples to watch with
him at Gethsemane, he found that they could not watch
even for one hour. Each time he returned they were asleep
"for their eyes were heavy" (Luke 22:46).

   We know that sleep as inertia can represent resistance

The illustration contains the following text within it:

MUTUS LIBER, IN QUO TAMEN
tota Philosophia herme *tica, figuris hieroglyphicis*
depingitur, ter optimo *maximo Deo misericordi*
consecratus, solisque *filiis artis dedicatus,*
authore cuius nomen *est Altus.*
21. 11. 82. *Neg:*
93. 82. 72. *Neg:*
82. 81. 33. *Tued.*

Angels awakening a sleeper for the journey, from the Mutus liber.
(Reprinted from The Golden Game *by Stanislas Klossowski de Rola,
courtesy George Braziller, Inc.)*

to change. In this sense we tend to resist awakening and this is why we need initiation to move psychic energy that is "stuck." There is in us a strong urge to defend ourselves against change until a force stronger than our defense displaces it. But this movement is always felt like a death threat to our ego. In other words, as much as we may want to change, there seem to be forces within us saying, "No!" Sleep as inertia, whatever form that may take in our own experience, can deaden the possibility and risk of growth, substituting the comforts of illusion. Awakening can be a truly frightening experience. But initiations ground us in the archetypal world which supports us, as a felt sense of that immortal quality which infuses and makes meaningful our daily life.

The Advent call is repeated, "Awake! Your salvation is near" (Romans 13). In Hebrew the word for salvation, *yasha,* means "to be wide, spacious . . . to develop without hindrance."[3] It implies a progressive loosening and freeing from constriction, from "dis-ease." In religious terms salvation is experienced as grace, a gift that opens us to an awareness of our potential and of life's meaning because we are sharers in the divine nature. Psychologically, viewed in terms of psychic birth, salvation refers to the possibility of freeing imprisoned feelings and emotions.

What follows in the Advent texts, however, does not, at first, seem to have anything in common with grace or salvation:

> The powers of heaven will be shaken . . . There will be signs in the sun and moon and stars: on earth nations in agony, bewildered by the clamour of the ocean and its waves . . . and then they will see the Son of Man coming in a cloud with power and great glory (Luke 25–28).

Before the Flood people were eating, drinking, taking wives, taking husbands right up to the day Noah went into the ark, and they suspected nothing until the flood came and swept all away. It will be like this when the Son of Man comes (Matthew 24:37).

What can we make of these catastrophic scenes appearing as they do at the beginning of a season that prepares for birth? On one level both of these texts are related to the cosmogonic myth that relates how the world, as well as each of us, is born, develops, weakens, dies and is reborn. Biblically, apocalyptic scenes of world destruction always point to a re-creation and a new existence basically different from the old. Life is lived on a new level since the old order has been destroyed.

It is known that in pre-psychotic patients, dreams of world destruction may point to imminent collapse of an enfeebled ego. But such images may also point to the possibility of a dramatic shift in consciousness. What appears in the psychotic as an exaggerated form of the destruction-order motif is present in every "normal" development of consciousness. Destruction and death in dreams and in conscious life often reflect the chaos of endings, followed by new beginnings. "Chaos," writes Jung, "is the *sine qua non* of any regeneration of the spirit and personality."[4] Psychologically viewed, these two readings describe the shattering movement of differentiation from the archetypal world. In personal experience, this can take many forms. When a baby is born he or she suffers from the "disordering" effects of leaving the womb and coming into earth. Ideally these effects are modified or absorbed by the mother through her holding and mirroring. But if a baby has to cope with too much disorder it will have difficulty developing its own inner "ordering principle" and will most likely experience as an adult great anxiety in facing the unknown.

But in any coming into awareness, as we take back a projection, or as we begin to experience new self-awareness, we come closer to our own vulnerability and our world may be shaken. There may be a sense of no *terra firma*. The two Advent texts describe cosmic destruction. In the first, the sun and moon no longer give their light, for "the powers of heaven are shaken." On earth "nations are bewildered and in agony." In the second text, desolation is felt when all seems swept away as if by flood. In antiquity the flood was an image for ignorance of and alienation from God and from the Self. The symbolism of water as both life-giving and destructive is reflected in the biblical view of the deluge as a type of baptism. In the midst of the turmoil described in these texts, the Son of man appears.

It has been said that these readings were included at masses celebrated by Pope Gregory the Great on one Sunday late in November when Rome was being devastated by floods and storms. His purpose was to reassure the people that even in the midst of such natural disasters, God was with them. A later scribe apparently kept the readings as a part of the Advent cycle, though it is not certain whether Gregory intended this. The God who is present in the storm appears as Son of man.

Son of man is a title that refers to Christ both as a heavenly divine figure and as a lowly servant. In Ezekiel 7: 26, Deuteronomy 7:13, and the apocryphal vision of Enoch, the title is interpreted as the divinity which incarnates, moving closer and closer to human form. Jung connects the Son of man figure to the Self. Psychologically this figure does not correspond to Christ but to the archetypal predisposition that enabled the human race to accept Christ. This predisposition is, in Jung's view, the longing or desire for wholeness. Another representation of this longing is the Greek *Anthropos,* which means "humanity." "Son of man" or *Anthropos* corresponds to the "human-divine" core of our personality, the voice of the authentic self.

We can say that flood and cosmic destruction point to a regression of energy back to the possibility of a new beginning, the *illo tempore* in which *Anthropos*/Son of man energies are stirred up. This observation is borne out clinically in work with persons who feel the chaos of their emptiness and who, in searching for their authenticity, unconsciously seek stimulation through addiction to food, drugs, knowledge, perfectionism or the pursuit of the "winning image." In these people, and to some degree in all of us, there is a resistance to the inner world of the unconscious. And yet, as the biblical texts point out, it is precisely during moments of inner chaos that the Self sends us dreams or other manifestations of its presence. A client who had recently attempted suicide dreamed: "I am in a hospital ward. I have become a child again and I am in the ward to start my life from the beginning."[5] In this dream, as Edinger points out, the image of child represents the *prima materia,* the return to pure potentiality with the prospect of a new self or a new attitude ready to emerge, a return to the unconscious for rebirth or renewal.

To summarize thus far, we have suggested that of the images central in the biblical texts of the first week of Advent, the mountain is the setting where the action unfolds, for the Cosmic Mountain is the Center of the World where creation begins. Destruction precedes creation as death precedes birth. In a psychological context we can say that any birth into consciousness is accompanied by varying degrees of disorientation and chaos. The ego must be strong enough to "hold" the effects of movement into "birth." We resist consciousness as we resist giving up the status quo; we resist psychic birth as we fear leaving Paradise. The paradox of dying and awakening is aptly expressed by Emily Dickinson:

> A death-blow is a life blow to some
> Who, till they died, did not alive become;
> Who, had they lived, had died, but when
> They died, vitality begun.[6]

In the process of coming to psychic birth the "death" blow can refer to the separation from the paradisical "sleep" or the protection of the false self. Clinically we see this as a gradual movement in which the unconscious, which wants to be "incarnated" guides us on the way. Let us now look in some detail at this process of waking up as it began to happen in a man I will call Edward.

Edward had difficulty in forming a long-term relationship with a woman and this is what led him into therapy. Jungian analysis also interested him because, in his words, of its "mystical" quality and because he was fascinated by the theory of archetypes. Edward had had a dream two months before he came to my office. In that dream he was telephoning his mother from an underground cave. The cord on the phone was very long and he said that it reminded him of an umbilical cord. During our third session Edward showed me a picture he had painted of a recent dream image. In the center of the page he had sketched a mouth partially open and across it in bold letter he had printed the word FREEDOM. At the top of the picture he had sketched the figure of Brigitte Bardot in an erotic pose. At the bottom of the picture appeared many animals, walruses, giraffes, etc.

The word, Freedom, appeared in the dream because of

his desire to be free, Edward offered. The mouth reminded him of his mother, whom he remembered as two-sided. By this he meant that she had a smiling face and a stern face. He breathed more freely when she smiled, and tailored his behavior accordingly. A quiet and well-behaved child, Edward became an excellent student. It was, however, the fear of the destructive side of the Mother archetype that Edward needed to wrestle with if he would get to the other side of his rather passive personality. After all, the mouth does represent orality and an oral attitude toward life is one of receptivity and passivity. Was there a side of Edward that wanted to be free, but through a passive attitude rather than through his own action? This remained to be seen. We use our teeth to chew and assimilate food. For Edward study, "assimilating" concepts gave a feeling of freedom. He had difficulty with his feelings and with sensation. On one level he wished to be free from earthy, body, instinct and the concrete reality of dealing with daily life. On another level, he longed for this contact, for the "birth" of this aspect of his personality. Yet he feared it, as it represented for him constriction and limitation.

Other significant images in his picture included the sketch of Brigitte Bardot at the top of the page representing the spirit world or Edward's fantasy life. Bardot is dressed in black, indicating that the reality of woman, that is, his relation to his own anima is still somewhat unconscious. In contrast, at the bottom of the picture the animals represent a phallic quality, especially the giraffes. He paints the animals orange, the color of Mars and of conflict, representing, perhaps, his conflict with his earthly masculine qualities, his sexuality and his aggressivity. Early on in therapy we did not discuss any of these associations as it was necessary simply to follow the unconscious and to "wait." We put the picture aside and as the weeks passed Edward brought dreams in which he was performing dangerous feats to the applause of a large audience. We talked about fantasies and Edward admitted that the reason he left his good position as an architect was that he had had a fantasy about being tops in that profession. When the fantasy had not been realized, he left and returned to the university to study. Gradually he began to see that his grandiose fantasies protected him from deep feelings of his own worthlessness. He began to "descend" into his own *nigredo*.

Edward began to face some of his fears and began to struggle with anger with his parents and with his boss. He began to develop a relationship with a new woman, Mary, and eventually moved into an apartment with her, a big step for him since his mother strongly disapproved. Mary supported him in his religious aspirations, his need for meditation and times of retreat. Yet there were arguments over sharing daily chores such as shopping, cleaning, cooking which Edward felt were "women's work." These arguments brought out feelings of "wanting to be taken care of." Mary was helping to bring him into the world of daily living where he, too, needed to take responsibility for such mundane tasks as emptying the garbage. Clearly Edward was drawn to the spirit world, and while Mary valued this in him, she was quick to "call him back" when she felt he was not being present to her.

Another aspect of Edward's fascination with the spirit world had to do with his creative intuition and a giftedness that also came from his closeness to the Mother world. One day he brought this dream:

> I take out a case of big crystals. Some are transparent—like glass—with a red core. Others are blue and yellow. One is like a chestnut with a brown covering or husk with an amethyst stone. I want to own it. But I'm con-

scious of dreaming and wonder whether this crystal really exists.

Then I'm in a cave sitting against a wall. The cave is wide and wet. I feel unprotected against animals but, at the same time, sheltered. I reflect on how our ancestors lived here.

There is another room underground with what looks like a glass surface. First I see one person pursuing another as if gliding on ice. They seem like thin pale lifeless figures with painted (masklike) faces gliding over the surface floor.

In this dream Edward had the impression of living in another reality. He was struck, first of all, by the crystal. "I could take it in my hand, but in the dream I know I'm not the owner." The red core referred, he thought, to his sexuality which he wants to be more in touch with. The pale figures beneath the earth look to him like El Greco figures.

We might say that in this dream the case as "container" may represent the Self, the container of all forms that organize our psychic functioning. The colored crystals—red, blue, yellow—could represent various aspects of feeling that range from the instinctive to the spiritual side, the amethyst or purple representing the union of instinct and spirit, enclosed in the brown husk, which might be see as life-giving and related to earth. The crystal here may relate both to Edward's sexuality and to his longing for the transcendent, two aspects of one reality.

In the second part of the dream the cave may correspond in the realm of nature to what is shown in the first part—the realm of spirit. In contrast to the dreams in which Edward is performing before an audience, here he sits in a bare damp cave unprotected against the animals and reflecting on the ancestors. Here he comes to a truer attitude for being open to spiritual values. He is humbled and in touch with his authentic self. In the underground the gliding figures seem to represent Mercurial figures, as the alchemists would say, an earthy "light," "gods" living in the depths of the earth, and in ourselves.

Many dreams followed during the next year. In one Edward was attacking his boss with a sword. In another he was in his parents' home defecating in his parents' bed. These are images of rebellion and aggression. Gradually Edward began to take a stand and to speak up for himself. After a meeting with his boss during which he was able to air his grievances, he said he felt "free." Then there was a series of dreams in which Edward was reprimanded by a judge or was condemned to death by a jury. These dreams often followed instances when he had failed to live up to his own expectations. Once, for example, he led a tour in an art museum. He was not speaking his native tongue. Realizing afterwards that he had made some grammatical errors, he mulled over these on his way home. The more he thought about it the more negative he felt about his whole performance. He then became a failure and furthermore, he was no good. During these times when his inner "critic" condemned him, he could find no good in himself. It was as if he were condemned to death.

His dreams began to change in tone as he gradually responded both to the inner figures and to the people in his daily life, especially to Mary. Edward had paid little attention to his nutrition and to exercise. He preferred the sedentary life, and was somewhat overweight. Now, at Mary's prodding, he began to do some exercise in a disciplined way, and began occasionally to prepare simple meals. Once on his return from a retreat he informed me that he had set the table and worked in the kitchen during the week and had really enjoyed it!

Edward began to feel better about his life. He was still living with Mary, and he felt freer about having taken a stand against his mother regarding that relationship and about his affiliation with the church. Though deeply religious, Edward had moved away from the institutional church and his guilt over this began to subside. At other times he appeared "down," and during these times we would reflect on what happened. Often this mood was triggered by a criticism by his professor or by Mary. A paper was not considered good enough; Edward's "inner critic" would tell him, "You're no good." Mary complained that he spent more time on retreats and workshops than with her. This raised issues over his sexuality and ability to maintain a relationship. Again the "inner critic" pounced. When Edward began to realize the power of this "critic" and began to connect with another side in him who could accept him for himself, he found some balance again and a perspective on both his limitations and his giftedness.

Toward the end of our work together Edward brought this dream:

> I am in a house where I used to rent an apartment. Some people there approach me carrying a little baby. It is grey in color and hardly recognizable as human. There is a doctor there who tells me I am to be responsible for the baby. The doctor tells me to go shopping for apples. I am to feed the apples to the baby.

Analysands often associate "baby" in a dream to the divine child. Edward wondered whether this were a "divine child." Often when we have a neglected child within, we tend to sublimate, to make the baby "divine." This dream baby represents a new possibility for potential growth in Edward and it is in need of air and nourishment. It is Edward's responsibility. We talked about food and nourishment and his own lack of attention to his eating habits in terms of balance and nutrition, part of his difficulty with sensation and relating to his body. He remembered his mother preparing meals for the family but often not having enough time to sit down and eat with them. Sharing meals with others is sharing oneself with them. And Edward was aware of his need for emotional nourishment. The dream suggests that he needs to nourish himself.

There is much archetypal imagery around apples as food of the gods, the basic food related to Demeter, the Earth Goddess. Apples are related to vegetation, earth, body. There is a tradition that apples, symbols of eros and relatedness were given at Halloween as expressions of wishing fertility on the receiver. In the dream going to shop for ordinary apples indicates going into the ordinary world to buy food, prepare it and feed the baby. True, in reality Edward did not like shopping. The dream touches a side of him that prefers to be passive in the mother world and to be cared for by others. The dream indicates, perhaps, that Edward's development leads him to a positive experience of God or the Self, not by separating from the world, but by going into it. Fuller insertion into the everyday reality and working to nourish himself is his path to "incarnation."

Once we can begin to feel our own "earth," our own body and begin to care for and nourish ourselves, we can more easily begin to relate to our unconscious side. Edward seemed on the way toward awakening to psychic birth of his real self, which for him would entail the balancing of his "highs" and "lows" and the reconnection to his inner value or Self. Awakening to psychic birth is likened here to a separation from "Paradise" or original state of union, in Edward's case expressed in the first dream image of the telephone cord and umbilical cord. It is more exciting and dramatic to stay in a "participation mystique" with the archetype, to "feel" the containment and comfort of Paradise, fascinated by our dream images without really relating to them. It is painful to separate from Paradise, to disidentify with the archetype and to consciously relate to it. This entails taking back our projections on others. For example, Edward began to sense that his anger with the boss had to do with his own anger at giving over his power to the "boss." He needed to reclaim his own anger and his own inner authority. The more we have suffered as infants and children, the more difficult it is to reclaim our emotions so that we may more easily bear the tension of relating to others and to the "world." It feels better to "stay in" Paradise.

Our journey toward fuller consciousness leads us to separate from a regressive Paradise to move toward the Paradise of the future, called in the Bible the kingdom of God. Here in the first reading is imaged the gathering of all people streaming to the mountain where life is lived in harmony. In Isaiah's vision conflictual forces are pictured as having been reconciled:

> [People] will hammer their swords into ploughshares, their spears into sickles. Nations will not lift sword against nation, there will be no more training for war (Isaiah 2:4).

But this vision is a goal. Psychologically viewed, the movement out of the "uroboric" Paradise toward consciousness involves our projecting shadow, and projection isolates us because we project our own shadow onto the other. Our relationships, then, become to some degree illusory since the "other" carries parts of our own psyche. If we are to move toward wholeness we have tasks to perform. And chief among these is the task of relating to our shadow. We have seen that when an infant senses the environment as unwelcoming to the "power" and "divine energies" it brings into the world, it will grow up feeling that others and the world are essentially inimical to its growth. A child who is welcomed shows no destructive aggressivity; one who is rejected begins to harbor destructive rage gradually projected onto others. This part of the journey, the recovery of our shadow energies, leads us to the wilderness, another chapter in the Advent liturgy.

For now, in summary, we have seen that the opening Advent texts are rich in archetypal imagery which evoke in us a personal initiation experience into rebirth or into birth. During the first week the image of the mountain recalls the *axis mundi* or Center of the World where re-creation can occur. Here in the time before creation, Spirit and Earth are joined, the temple above and the temple or oven of incubation within. The call of Advent as an awakening initiates a breakthrough in consciousness, and with it a period of chaos and disorder. Images of destruction often accompany such an awakening. Only when we feel the chaos of our own vulnerability does the Son of man appear as a stabilizing center. God is present in the chaos and the depression. It would seem that Edward experienced some of this energy when he dreamed how he found himself in a cave sitting against a wall feeling unprotected against the animals but, at the same time, sheltered.

This image would describe, it would seem, a "coming to oneself." It is an awakening to hope. The repeated regression or merging with the Self and its manifestation in emotional highs and lows presents the first and longest challenge in therapy leading to psychic birth. It is the way of many "deaths" that can lead us to the child of exuberance and joy. Perhaps this explains why both the second and third week of Advent focus on the Baptist and the wilderness. The beginnings of self-discovery are often experienced, as the Gnostics say, "in anguish and terror . . . in pain and confusion . . . in a kind of roadlessness, and not knowing where to go."[7] When we face our anguish and terror we can begin to experience our anger and gradually to reclaim it. For underneath our fear we often hide our power; paradoxically, a power that we fear. This is especially true if we, as children, feared our parents. In moving toward psychic birth we need our anger to help us to reclaim our power, our power to love and to create. Our anger is the fiery fuel of transformation, and it is the wilderness background imaged now in the Advent liturgy that, in a psychological context, provides the "container" for this transformation process.

5

Anger

In T.S. Eliot's *The Cocktail Party* the psychiatrist speaking to a young woman patient says:

> (The Way) is unknown and so requires faith
> the kind of faith that issues from despair.
> The destination cannot be described.
> You will know very little until you get there.
> You will journey blind. But the way leads
>   towards possession
> Of what you have sought for in the wrong place.[1]

The way leads to separation and to reunion; in the context of psychic birth, separation from the "participation mystique" and return to the unconscious as source of renewal. The feelings that accompany this movement of separating the "I" from the "not I," feelings of confusion and chaos, are experienced whenever we move significantly to a new level of consciousness. We are frightened and we do not know where to go; "we travel blind." To be in the wilderness is to be in transition. Like the Israelites who, freed from the slavery of Egypt but not yet arrived in free territory, we know the uncertainty when, at times, going back to the old looks more inviting than risking the unknown of the new. There is no other way during these times of transition, whether we find ourselves in a therapeutic situation or not, than to go through the wilderness. For within its darkness lie buried the seeds of life.

It may seem strange to us that during Advent the way leads to the wilderness. A bleak and sterile looking place, the wilderness does not look like an appropriate setting for birth. On the contrary, the wilderness is associated with conflict, confrontation, and struggle. There dwell evil spirits (Luke 8:29) and demonic powers (Deuteronomy 8:15). And what do conflict and struggle with "evil" spirits have to do with "birthing"? Simply everything. Psychically if we are to "feel" this inner child as "self," that is, if the child is to be embodied, it must come through the wilderness. The child as symbol of inner strength and confidence is the fruit of the struggle. Without the confrontation with our own "demons" our "child" will be experienced in a mystical or spiritual way, as "air," and not "fire," as "out there," not within.

Fire and water are the elements of the Advent wilderness. Fire represents anger, rage, passion, love; water, the life principle of birth. Psychologically we know that often our fire lies buried under depression. Though we may have been forced in childhood to repress it, our fire is our friend. In the wilderness we may recover the fire of our anger at family, institutions, or society, and, more importantly, at ourselves. Our anger, then, can transform and give meaning to our birth into our biological family and reveal to us our transcendent destiny as children of God. Our psychic child often comes to birth as we struggle with our anger. In this chapter we will explore the wilderness in some of its personal meanings as a place "in-between," as a place of vulnerability, as a place of struggle with our demons, and as the site of the new revelation or birth.

As "container" or "vessel" the wilderness becomes a metaphor for the circular *vas* to which heat was applied while the alchemist watched the mystery of creation happen again. It is as if in the wilderness we encounter again the *prima materia* or the original chaos, and the *nigredo,* the destruction and death by water and by fire. These images portrayed endings of one kind of existence, of one level of consciousness, and the awakening to another. Every such movement is a kind of birth and strengthening of the ego. But the "return" to the source of life is a progression on the way to birth if the ego is strong enough to descend into the unconscious, the darkness which it fears. Instead of death it may find there a "self" waiting to be born. The wilderness provides a holding frame, a barrier against becoming lost in the chaos, even though within that frame we can experience some of our own inner chaos. The frame or vessel will hold the heat, allowing it to change our darkness into light, our "unformed-ness" into solid earth.

Turning to the liturgical texts during the second week of Advent, we hear a "voice" calling out to us:

> A voice cries in the wilderness
> Prepare a way for the Lord.
> (Mark 1:2, Second Sunday of Advent)

Psychologically viewed, the voice calls from the unknown to the unknown. It is a call to trust in the sacred purpose of our life. For Jung this is our highest calling . . . fidelity to the law of our being. For the word "vocation" in its original sense means "to be addressed by a voice."[2] If we have suffered from physical or emotional abandonment in any form, we grow up feeling that we have not been "called." Jung pointed out that when we hear voices in dreams these come from the deeper layers of the psyche and must be taken seriously. For example, an analysand heard a clear voice in a dream, "I am going to rip your conscience to shreds." This woman realized only later that her "false" conscience, formed by an overly strict upbringing, faulted her own sexuality and growth into wholeness. Hearing a voice in dreams may indicate our readiness to approach unknown aspects of ourselves and to be receptive to their message.

The voice from the wilderness calls us to a new level of consciousness, and thus it places demands on us to follow our own path and to separate ourselves for a time from the conventions of society. The root of the words "desert" or "wilderness" means "to separate," "solitary." In nonbiblical Greek the word can also mean "to hand over," or "to set free." The darkness of *nigredo* feels like wilderness without connection, without hope. If we are on the way to birth of a sense of self our ability to relate to our inner world is disturbed, because we must contend with extremely negative voices coming from within. In the isolation of the wilderness, however, the inner voices that serve our life must be heard over those inner voices that seek to stifle it. It is the "old" worn-out attitudes that constrict us and turn our energies into negative forces. Symbolically, the Baptist as voice calls us into the future. He is an agent of change and risk and, as prophet, he embodies hope in the future.

John the Baptist appears on the Advent landscape as both an historical and a symbolical figure. As for the historical details of his life and death, we have few. In the fourth gospel his death is not mentioned and what we read about his birth is similar to the accounts foretelling the birth of Jesus. Both births are announced by the angel Gabriel and the names given to each child are divinely chosen. The Baptist is a "bridge" who links the old order of

Judaism and the new messianic kingdom of Christ. He himself belongs to neither. Intuiting the new or not yet realized, his presence stirs hope in his followers. In some sense the Baptist mirrors the deep longing of the people, holding up to them the image of Christ, and though they begin to mistake him for the messiah, the Baptist insists that he is only the "voice" in the wilderness. Yet beyond speech he leads his listeners through their fears and insecurities onto new ground, to the One who, already in their midst, remains unknown to them.

Beyond the historical dimension of his life, we can view the Baptist as an inner figure or a psychic function. In this sense the Baptist represents an energy that moves us into the future. According to Diel, there are certain periods of history characterized by sterility and decadence that cry out for voices of hope. Such was the Roman Empire before the birth of Christ and such is our own. During these times extraordinary persons appear who are animated by an exceptional vital impulse to bring harmony and renewal.[3] Hope is immanent to human life from the beginning, an evolutionary hope that periodically is stirred up and personified in a person. Historically this hope was personified in the Baptist, who called his followers to envision a new social order. As a psychic function we can view the Baptist as if he actually had appeared in one of our dreams. There he might function as an inner impulse or movement within ourselves, or he might represent an outer event, word, or person that stimulates life within us, and helps us to awaken from sleep, inertia, or depression, or from a gnawing sense that we are not living our own life. Following this inner vital impulse helps us to recover soul if we can begin to trust enough to listen to the voice of the child within us that hopes, the "eternal something" in us always becoming and never completed that wants to incarnate.

The Baptist, then, as voice, prophet, and vital impulse of hope becomes our Advent guide into the transition time, the "betwixt and between" time of initiation where we begin to work through the alchemical stages of chaos-conflict-creation. If our journey toward consciousness leads us into psychotherapy or Jungian analysis, we enter a structure and a relationship that evokes remembering and reliving childhood memories. We return to the past as an inner stage whose characters stir up old and new emotions. For those whose trust has been betrayed in childhood, entering this drama and this relationship provokes anxiety and they unconsciously and sometimes consciously protect themselves from experiencing anger, hatred, as well as love, for the analyst. Yet if the drama can be lived, it may lead to an experience of the "in-between" and the "time-in-and-out-of-time" of the wilderness experience.

Psychologically another aspect of the "in-between" time of the wilderness can be seen as the bridging of the emotional highs and lows we may experience. The source of these emotional swings goes back to a need to protect our weak vulnerable self. In doing so we unconsciously tend to feign greatness. Grandiosity needs to be "seen" or to fantasize being applauded for great intellectual achievements or for beauty or talent. If we feel cut off and empty inside we can maintain a sense of worth by excelling, by being tops in our academic or professional world. We may then take pride in having no need of others, while ourselves becoming a pillar of strength for the weak. In caring for others, we may be caring for our own needy side, while, at the same time receiving needed energy and recognition. Failure to receive needed emotional supplies may lead to depression, for our grandiose "self-confidence" can be very fragile. This is seen clearly in a dream of a female patient: "A balloon . . . it flew high in a good wind but then suddenly got a hole and soon lay like a little rag on the ground. . . ."[4]

Miller suggests that the crumpled balloon describes the sense of fragmentation suffered following a slight, or criticism, or a failure to receive needed admiration, attention, or empathy. The "in-between" time of the wilderness may be a time to begin resisting compulsive "doing" in order to better listen to our heart and to accept our vulnerability as a source of strength. It may be a time, too, to work at "leveling" or balancing as we become aware of events in daily situations that send us high or low.

The wilderness as the in-between time can also be viewed as a phase of the therapeutic process. For if as children we have not been "heard" or if, our needs have otherwise not been met, we grow up feeling we have no vocation, we have not heard a "call" for our life, there seems to be no plan for us that inspires our enthusiasm. Many analysands speak about a sense of "deadness" and "cut-offness." But during the in-between time of analysis, if all goes well, something "new" is on the way. It is as if we are in a period of "not yet," an unfolding of personality that, in its mystery, affects both analysand and analyst. It is as if a sense of I/Self exists between them appearing and disappearing within their interaction. During this time the analyst provides and nourishes the hope nascent within the psyche and, indeed, often becomes the personification of that hope. Thus the wilderness experience as a time in-between can be linked to a time during which the true self gradually makes it appearance, and the analysand begins to feel more inner stability or more "ground" within.

As the capacity for self-reflection increases, the wilderness boundaries serve as a place for exploring the other side of the ego or personal identity. As an aspect of our inner self the Baptist knows this side. Historically the Baptist preached that the kingdom of God must be open to everyone, rich and poor alike. And then, as now, his message to the establishment was disturbing:

> John the Baptist found a means by which the common folk and other "sinners" who because of laxness in regard to the demands of the Law were regarded as ritually and morally "unclean" could be regenerated apart from the meticulous observance of the Law . . . John must be credited with initiating ministry to the "poor."[5]

Would the injustice against the poor which we experience in the outer world change if, psychically, we could more fully accept our inner "poor"? It is here that we fear the ambivalence of the wilderness; for to be in this place is to feel weak and vulnerable. The Baptist accepts all the people ordinarily rejected, that is, considered inferior, because they have failed to live up to the standards of the Law. John's following, as we know, included many outcasts of the day, harlots (Matthew 21:32), soldiers (Luke 3:14), and the hated tax collectors (Luke 3:12).

But to accept our own "poor" and to look at the shabby and petty parts of ourselves, as well as at the sad and lonely parts, is intolerable if our trust has been betrayed earlier in life. We cannot let ourselves experience weakness. And this defense against experiencing weakness and vulnerability merely fortifies the pattern of denial, suppression and depression. Contempt for the weakness of others, then, becomes the best defense against the realization of our own. Jung sees the individuation process as the reconciliation of opposites, and the Self as the Center that accepts all that we are, our meanness and envy as well as our generosity and goodness. A symptom of damage to the ego's connection with the Self is the lack of self-acceptance. If there is no healthy tension of opposites, often the case when feeling and emotion have been split off and repressed, both the ego and Self are weakened. The Self may be experienced as a symbolic reality but not as a companion and inner guide.[6] We begin to shun our weakness for we feel that we must be strong. Then we may say, "I must do things myself; I don't need anybody." This masculine force crushes the feminine possibility for relatedness to our vulnerability and to the Self, and it fosters a kind of masochistic attitude toward the self. To recover access to instinct, and to our real needs, we must first experience our demons.

Now we come to the third heading under which we look at the meaning of wilderness, as a place where we struggle with the demons. Biblically, the wilderness is associated with conflict. Evil and demonic spirits dwell there (Luke 8:29). Christ confronted Satan in the wilderness and struggled with the demonic powers. Later Christian tradition taught that these forces have been "conquered" by Christ. But the dark forces are not in opposition to God, but rather aspects of the spirit. The demons want to be religiously taken into account by us. Psychologically, demons and evil spirits are connected to the "dead" and to the ancestors, that is, to our unrealized unconscious creativity.

Psychologists tell us that adults who grow up split off from the spontaneity and sense of body they had as children often dreamed that they were dead: "I am lying on my bed. I am dead. My parents are talking and looking at me but they don't realize that I am dead."[7] If these children can recover the fire and life hidden beneath the feeling of deadness they can begin to balance the highs and lows or the grandiose and depressive poles of their emotional suffering. An important aspect of the "way" to psychic birth consists of finding equilibrium or balance between these highs and lows. Confronting the weak despised sides of ourselves is difficult enough for us even if we have grown up in a loving and supportive environment, but failing this, we tend to split off our shadow, and with that, as Jung says, we lose a feeling of connection with our body. How we experience our body derives in large measure from how as babies we were held and soothed, accepted and loved. If we have not experienced these enough, we tend to repress sensation and instinctual responses. The body becomes the personification of the shadow.

To recover our self and our body is to recover our inner "fire," or our anger. It is with the animal powers that we often associate fire in both its demonic and divine sense. In many cultures the animal was divinized. The Egyptians worshipped the cat god, Bastet, and in the Greek cult of healing the temple of Aesculapius housed live serpents, for the serpent represented wisdom, healing, and rebirth. Often in fairy tales and dreams animals appear to help the hero or the dreamer out of a difficult situation. Animals in fairy tales may also represent "bewitched" sides of our personality that want to be freed. It is known that our culture generally fails to honor and value animals, and this says much about our contact with our own instinctual nature, our "earth" and our body. Animals, unlike human beings, do not act against their own nature. Caged, neglected animals become dangerous. From a psychological perspective Nietzsche writes:

> If you fulfill the pattern that is peculiar to yourself you have loved yourself... You have abundance. If you hate yourself you have not accepted your pattern... there are hungry animals, prowling cats and other beasts in your constitution seeking to satisfy their appetites...[8]

It is by approaching our "animals" that we can begin to get in touch with our own pattern, our own "true" self. If we have unconsciously locked up our wounded "poor sides," we have some hungry and destructive animals inside.

Psychologically, then, the wilderness provides a space where we can begin to integrate these shadow "animal" energies. As we have seen, the shadow is the other side of the developing ego, containing those qualities we did not use or could not express as we grew into adulthood. In the psychically "unborn" personality the shadow is dominated by rage and envy. From an archetypal viewpoint, rage is motivated by early injury done to the self. There has been a tampering with the connection to the Self-Image and this means a tampering with the nascent development of the child's personality. The healthy parts of the personality respond with rage to the experience of "psychic rape," but repress the rage out of fear.[9] As a result we feel victimized by an overpowering masculine force that makes demands on us to be perfect, on the one hand, and on the other, to repress our real needs and desires. We are caught, then, in a place that stifles the flame that transforms us, often hiding under our sadness and depression.

When there is a strong resistance to "going into" our depressive feelings, the resistance must be taken seriously by both therapist and analysand. Our guidance often comes from our dreams. Sara, a twenty-two-year-old analysand of mine was not suffering from great emotional swings, but she complained about her lack of confidence, and her fear that she would never be able to relate to men. Sara's parents were divorced when she was eleven and she lived with her mother, an alcoholic. She remembered her father as irascible and unapproachable, though as she grew older she longed to have a relationship with him and was angered that she had been assigned the role of go-between between him and her mother. Sara often seemed "down" in spite of the fact that she did well at the university and was on her way to becoming an accomplished artist.

During our third session she brought the following dream:

> There was a great hall made of marble. A woman was lying in the middle of the floor. She was attractive, wearing a soft white dress. She rose slowly, turning around faster and faster and turning into what looked to me like a white disc. She was called Christiana and someone says a friend of mine wants to marry her.

Out of fear Sara, from childhood, had adapted to what had been expected of her. The dream indicates that, for her, the search for her own identity is central. The great hall of marble reminds us of the great temple of the goddesses, perhaps relating to her unconscious fantasy of herself. The lovely woman rises slowly, swirling all the while, reminiscent of the dervish religious dance in which the dancers circle around and move toward a "centering." Wearing a soft white dress, the dream-ego is a picture of feminine gracefulness. The white disc may represent the centering aspect of the personality, the Self. The dream ends with a suggestion of a future positive union with the creative animus.

Three months later Sara brought this dream:

> There was a hotel or a castle with big rooms. It was dark. One room had a staircase beside it. I was in the room and don't know if my father was there. There were some other people. They felt someone was coming to kidnap me. I held on to a table so as not to be taken. Someone came and pulled me away . . . my arms and then my leg. They dragged me to the door but the table was too big to get through. But they pulled my leg and hurt it at the

hip. They caught me and took me away. The man took me to a restaurant and someone there, a girl, told me that it's better to smile and be friendly, to "bow" to the men.

My leg was hurting. Then I knew something terrible would happen. They took me away and I felt they would kill me. Then it was daylight and the man came. I hit him with a stick but only scratched the side of his face. He had blood on his head. I saw he wasn't dead and I hit him again and killed him and ran away.

Sara was sweating when she awoke. In the dream she felt that she had to kill the man. "It was the right thing to do." Much could be said about this dream, but what is of particular interest here is the wrestling with and, in this case, the killing of the negative masculine force. The incident recalls Jacob's wrestling with the angel which resulted in his wounded hip. The hip which is related to the genital area suggests a wounding of the instinct. Sara, in fact, idealized men and tried to gain a sense of her feminine identity by playing a role as their anima, by, as the dream figure suggests, "bowing" to the men.

We might say that in this dream by risking the fight, she had won—by anticipation—a victory over her lack of confidence, a victory gained through facing her own darkness. In so doing the way is opened toward recovering the positive animus, and hinted in Sara's initial dream, the true union and a greater sense of her own feminine identity. But the breaking away from these destructive forces feels like a wrenching of one's being. It is a struggle that is never once and for all completed. But we must make the choice of life over death with all that means in terms of struggle with our demons, over and over again. While the ego must assert itself against these negative forces we often feel that the unconscious "powers" are at times particularly menacing.

Envy is another side of the false-self demon that must be faced in the wilderness. Envy is experienced in actual relationships as well as in negative forces within. Sara, for example, was envied by her sisters and by some of the students at the university she attended. They envied her for her physical attractiveness, her artistic ability, her achievements. Yet she often felt that whatever she accomplished meant nothing, that she would never be successful in life. "Nothing good can happen to you, only to others." At times in the therapeutic process this inner envy turns into negative transference, since the analysand cannot feel that anyone could really care for her. Then, too, envy can kill off the nascent feelings of desire and the hopeful "child of joy" who seeks to be born in us. Jung was fond of saying that we do not transform the shadow by imagining figures of light but through experiencing the darkness. In Christian tradition, the experience of the inner divine child as the recovery of an aspect of our self is the fruit of the sojourn in the wilderness.

This explains why the wilderness was thought of as a place of revelation and a "holy" place. It was thought that the hope of salvation, the messiah, would come from the wilderness. In later Hebrew tradition the desert is the place where Israel is reunited to Yahweh. God speaks to her heart and "betroths" her. In St. Mark's gospel the wilderness and the Jordan River are identical. In the midst of the vast wilderness harboring fiery spirits and demons flows the river where John baptized. The destructive and regenerative properties of fire and water are well known. Fire represents warmth, vitality, sexuality, eroticism, passion, all related to earth energies. Fire also symbolizes mystical and spiritual energies. The Holy Spirit appears in tongues of fire. Unless we experience our own "fire" in the demons of our grief and rage within our body, we will not be strong enough to contain the joy and wonder of the new birth as our own.

Psychologically we need to make an important distinction here between the first stage of the spiritual journey, often referred to as "purification." In alchemy, as we have seen, the process of *calcinatio* consists in the fiery purification of ego desires. This is necessary in order to modify ego power demands and to "tame" passion. But in those on the way to psychic birth such attempts at purification sabotage the process, since felt needs, ego desires, and passion have been repressed or split off. To the contrary, practices of asceticism and purification may repeat an early pattern of denying the real self, thereby feeding an unconscious appetite for masochism. Then I deny to myself what had been denied me. Rather, it is through embodying our split-off emotions that we may begin to recover our inner fire and to sense our real needs as aspects of emerging creative energies imaged as the hidden repressed child. Analytically it is, of course, necessary for the personality to begin to hold the tension between legitimate needs and grandiose childish demands, and the analyst must frustrate the latter so that a realistic sense of the self can be internalized. The grandiose ego demands must decrease, as the self expressing its true needs and potential, increases.

The Baptist calls his followers to the river. "Why are you baptizing, if you are not the Christ?" (John 19:28, third Sunday of Advent.) Descent into the Jordan River represents a further movement into the feminine realm of the psyche. Here lies the focal point of our entrance into the initiatory darkness, but this darkness brings us closer to the realization of our authentic self. Eliade links this descent into darkness with hope:

Initiation lies at the core of any genuine human life. And this is true for two reasons. The first is that any genuine human life implies profound crises, ordeals, suffering, loss and reconquest of self, "death and resurrection." The second is that, whatever degree of fulfillment [life may have brought] at a certain moment [our] life seems a failure. This vision does not arise from a moral judgment made on the past, but from an obscure feeling that [we] have missed our vocation, or betrayed the best that was in us. In such moments of total crisis only one hope seems to offer any issue, the hope of beginning life over again . . . in a total renewal. . . .[10]

Baptism symbolizes a type of renewal that is the result of every religious conversion. Psychically the illuminative aspect of going down into the waters of baptism corresponds to the specific energy of the archetype which Jung calls the "numinosum." In religious terms it corresponds to a sense of awe in the presence of the divine. Its healing power comes from the fact that it is beyond an arbitrary act of will. For Jung it is the experience of the numinous that brings about the renewal.

In Christianity baptism recalls the deluge with its destruction . . . death . . . regeneration motif. Baptism symbolizes death to one level of existence. St. Paul calls it a "burial" with Christ. The alchemists referred to a rite of renewal in which the people were immersed in a crater containing "divine tinctures," a special kind of purifying element. It was believed that through the "dipping" they were transformed in a miraculous way into spiritual beings. The idea is similar to that found in Christianity, where the baptismal font as "womb" of mother church, fertilized by the Spirit, regenerates the initiates into their "divine" life. The new birth is conceived and nourished by divine, that is, archetypal "parenting." Psychologically John's baptism in the desert can represent a nascent positive experience of the Self and, along with this, the possibility of being "reparented." Baptism imagery during the third week of Advent may suggest to us that, as we are on the way to a "second birth," whatever lack we experience in our personal parents is filled out and transformed in the realization that from the depths of the divine a voice calls to us as it called to Jesus: "You are my beloved child."

Anthony Stevens writes that failure to receive adequate parenting when we needed it results in "parental hunger," the search for the ideal father, mother, or lover, an unattainable goal.[11] But the psyche heals, and as we descend into its waters, we can be compensated by the archetypal good mother and good father. As with all archetypes, Mother and Father show both a loving and a destructive face. The positive Mother is earth in its nurturing, creative aspect. This mother provides holding, cuddling, security, and comfort, while her destructive side smothers or abandons, or "uses" her children for her own comfort. The archetypal masculine is related to order, discipline, responsibility, and morality. Good fathers teach and support us so that we move more securely to find our place in the world, confident that we can master the tasks involved. If the real father has been physically or emotionally absent we know that there are available to us the archetypal "good" Father energies to compensate. If our mother has been domineering or "smothering," good Mother energies are available to us if we can begin to dialogue with our unconscious. We have the potential within us to contact these energies as we integrate our shadow grief and as we come to experience those "unborn" aspects of ourselves that now need "parenting."

Baptism carries the added significance already alluded

to when we spoke of the winter solstice festivals and the myth of eternal return. Baptism signifies the return to the womb for rebirth, back to the origins to regain a renewed consciousness, a renewed body, for returning to the water is returning to the place where we are in our natural rhythm. The wilderness is the place where our fire-demons give us their energy to work for us not against us. New life begins to quicken and leads to the capacity in us to hold tension that will help to strengthen our sense of self, to help balance our highs and lows. We need during these times of psychic change to be patient with ourselves for such change comes slowly.

A text from a letter of St. James sets the tone for this period of "waiting" during the third week of Advent:

> Be patient, brothers, until the Lord's coming. Think of a farmer: how patiently he waits for the precious fruit of the ground until it has had the autumn rains and the spring rains! You too have to be patient; do not lose heart, because the Lord's coming will be soon (James 5:7, 8, Third Sunday of Advent).

The alchemists, too, frequently wrote about the importance of patience: "He who does not possess the gift of patience," writes Morienus, "let him hold back his hand from the work."[12] It is masculine "ego power" that tries to force change. Pregnancy, the growth of organic life, related to the moon, is slow.

Attracting more followers, the Baptist continues to preach and to baptize. "What must we do (now)?" the people ask (Luke 3:10). The prophet sends them back to their homes and to their work, cautioning them to be honest and to share what they have with the poor. Psychologically, this

means that the nascent experience of the Self in the wilderness is to be lived, not in seclusion, but in our relationships
and in the tasks of daily life.

Sometime later, Herod's messengers confront John:

> Who are you? We must take back an answer to those
> who have sent us. What have you to say about yourself?
> . . . "I am . . . a voice that cries in the wilderness . . ."
> (John 19:29).

King Herod fears the Baptist's influence over the people, as
the collective always fears the prophets who initiate change,
who seek to move us forward into the new, since these threat-
en to destroy the old order. Herod, succumbing to Salome's
request for the Baptist's head, sends an order that he be
murdered, as earlier he had ordered his soldiers to seek and
to destroy the divine child.

We have looked at the wilderness as a turning point or
transition from *nigredo* darkness to the lightening of dawn.
The wilderness represents an in-between time and a time
when we struggle with forces that would rob us of our power.
The wilderness as a holy place is a place where the divine is
revealed. Psychologically viewed, the Baptist as voice calls
us into the wilderness as a way to fulfill the vision of our life
as a unique unfolding of God's incarnation. On the journey
toward psychic birth we need to attune our heart to this
voice, as this is the only way to recover our own. Representing a vital impulse of hope within us, the Baptist intuits a
future beyond what we may envision. As an in-between time
the sojourn in the wilderness represents a time when something new begins to develop within the interchange between
client and analyst. As a place in-between the wilderness
provides a space where we can experience our vulnerability,
our "poor" sides and where we are challenged to struggle

with our demons. In the wilderness the dead can begin to revive through our descent into the waters, and we are reminded that baptism is a call to descend into the waters of the unconscious to be reborn and reparented, to become "beloved" of God.

Finally, the voice in the wilderness always asks one question, "Who are you?" When we experience our wilderness we come face-to-face with God, the "mirror" of the Self. Recovery of our "true" self comes through the feminine self represented by Mary, who through her mirroring of God gave birth to the divine child. It is to the fourth week of the Advent liturgy and to these feminine energies of joy that we now turn.

6

Joy

As we approach the fourth week of Advent, the fire and water imagery of the wilderness appear more subtly textured. Water as dew falls gently on the earth in response to the opening plea of the liturgy: "Drop down dew ye heavens from above and let the skies pour down the Just One . . ." (Isaiah 45:8). Now if we have been able to integrate some of our shadow, our envy, rage, anger, and fear, these shadow qualities gradually begin to lose their negative hold on us. Their power can begin to work for us. The wilderness shadow fire can transform our capacity to feel desire and joy. Out of the fiery struggle with our wilderness demons issues the fire of our own being, a Dionysian quality that flows and dances with joy, celebrating our real self liberated. It is the underground "god" of passion and eros, this fire at the center of the earth, our own instinctual fire that is at the same time the fire of divine love. Between the opposites of fire and water there appear during the fourth week of Advent air and earth imagery, and the motifs of ascent and descent, heaven and earth, sun and moon predominate. These images and the energies they hold converge in the figure of Mary as virgin, who, receptive to the Spirit of God, conceives the child.

Mary represents the feminine side of God, the feminine self. In alchemical imagery Mary as *vas* or vessel is the "belly," the cave, the womb, that "round vessel" said to contain some "magical key which unlocked the closed doors of matter" in order to free the god concealed there.[1] In this sense Mary represents energies that free us from the burden of our past, opening up the passageway for new life to emerge. The wilderness experience of baptism, immersion in the waters of renewal, affirm us in our value as born of God. But now we are led to discover more personally the archetypal Mother in her life-giving reality. If we sense in ourselves potentials yet unborn, then it is the Mary energies within us that shelter and nourish these aspects of ourselves so that they may be brought to birth. We can ask ourselves what it would feel like to experience this psychic energy imaged as Mary. Mary may represent our growing capacity to be still and to let our "inner world" speak to us so that we may recover our real needs and wants. If we can begin to trust, we can become less fearful of entering into our unconscious and we can begin to feel the good "ground" within. We can begin to experience ourselves as more fully alive in body and spirit. We can allow the joy within us to awaken.

During the liturgy of the fourth week this awakening begins with the appearance of dew. "Drop down dew ye heavens." After the night, the dew freshens and restores. Entering silently, it announces the coming of dawn, the alchemical *albedo,* or whitening. The night is now illuminated by the moon, which signifies in the analytical process that unconscious contents begin to come into consciousness. The process of integration continues, and though our vision may not be clear, we move into another level of awakening where we begin to experience "birth" as embodying. In the Hebrew scripture dew signifies blessing on the living (Genesis 27:28), and regeneration for the dead:

Your dead will come to life,
Their corpses will rise;
. . .
For your dew is a radiant dew
And the land of ghosts will give birth.
(Isaiah 26:19)

Not only will the land of the dead revive, it will bring forth
new life, as the dew fertilizes the dry earth. In alchemy the
healing water as dew falls on the "dead" to awaken them.[2]
The alchemical sea dew, an analogy for the water of life,
binds up and heals. The Egyptian goddess Isis, called,
"Dew," personifies its healing power as she unifies the dis-
membered Osiris, joining what had been separated into a
unity.

Psychologically speaking, dew is related to our tears.
Tears, in expressing our grief and despair, open us to the
life-giving waters of the unconscious, penetrating and sof-
tening our blocked energies so that they may flow once
again, putting us in touch with our real self. Like the dew,
our tears bring us release and blessing. While clouds and
dew are associated with Spirit and Logos, in ancient times it
was the goddess who was venerated as the giver of rain and
dew. The moistening power of the Earth Goddess caused
green plants to appear on the earth. Here we are in the
realm of the ancient Moon Goddess who brings forth the
rain and fertilizes the earth. She was also believed to
produce the dew, as she brought the waters both from the
heavens and from the earth and as she brings forth from
within us the life-giving waters of our tears, as she "graces"
our creativity and our rebirth.

For the alchemists, dew is the healing water, sometimes
called "virginal" water. As the alchemists dissolved the substances in their round vessel, heated them and watched as

the vapors ascended and then descended as condensed vapor, they were fascinated. This fascination with the effect of fire on matter may seem strange to us but we must recall that for the alchemists these properties of matter were unknown. They saw the vapor as a form of the most subtle spirit in the form of a fluid which they called "eternal water," a miraculous substance with curative and fertilizing powers. As they watched the vapors ascend and descend as condensed vapor they noted a circular movement as well. It was to them as if matter became "spiritualized" as it ascended and circled within the vessel.

Into this circle they projected the idea of completion and wholeness, because what happened before their eyes represented a psychic "centering" process. For Jung, the center of the psyche is the Self, its ordering principle, and the journey toward wholeness presupposes the ascent to Spirit and the descent to earth. As with the alchemists, this upward and downward movement causes a circular movement as well. It is this "circling" around the Self that brings us to a gradual sense of centering in our own self-identity. This ascent and descent motif is central in alchemy and in the movement toward "psychic birth." In this context dew represents the union of heaven and earth, conscious and unconscious from which the "child" is born.

Let us look more closely at this ascent and descent motif. We have seen that in Christianity the incarnation of Christ is pictured as a descent from heaven. St. Basil says, "He bowed the heavens and came down."[3] Christ came down in secret, his coming was hidden, but to complete his work he ascended into heaven. He who descended ascended for our sake, "and a cloud received him out of their sight" (Acts 1:9). Redemption is complete only with the ascension, for only then can the Spirit descend. In contrast, in alchemy the ascent comes first and then the descent. We have seen that, for the alchemists, the "child" comes from below, from the earth. An alchemical text from the Middle Ages describes the "child" of the elements:

> Its father is the sun, its mother the moon; the wind hath carried it in his belly; its nurse is the earth. Its power is complete when it is turned towards the earth. It ascendeth from the earth to heaven, and descendeth again to the earth, and receiveth the power of the higher and lower things. So wilt thou have the glory of the whole world.[4]

The alchemists believed that if this "birth" could come to term within us it would conquer all our spiritual and bodily sickness. This "birth" becomes an immortal "medicine," a value beyond all values.

Psychologically viewed ascent and descent, above and below, up and down refer to the emotional balancing of the opposites. In our dreams this motif occurs in images of going up or down a hill, ascending or descending in an elevator, a balloon, an airplane. In images of ascent and descent the psyche expresses a movement toward balancing or equilibrium. In body psychotherapy as well, we speak of bringing "vertical" and "horizontal" energies into balance. We hear people complain of "living in their head," finding it difficult to relax, to unwind, to "come down." The body sends messages in psychosomatic symptoms to indicate the need to "ascend" to the pure airy heights, or to descend into the vegetative or "earthy" regions for more "grounding."

Another aspect of the ascent and descent motif is related to idealizing and mirroring. When we idealize someone we see only their goodness, intelligence, and other positive qualities. We do not see their negative or shadow sides. We know that children need to idealize their parents. "My parents are the greatest!" For a time parents must accept the child's idealization, for it is a "godlike" projection of the spirit and it helps the child to get in touch with his or her own developing spiritual center. The child also needs to be mirrored. When someone "mirrors" us we feel understood. It is as if the other can "get under our skin" and know how we feel. Mirroring is related to descent. When the child feels understood he or she feels more grounded, more embodied.

Nathan Schwartz-Salant has seen in the ascent and descent motif an analogy for the idealizing and mirroring transferences in the therapeutic process. For those on the way to psychic birth the therapy vessel becomes, like the alchemical *opus* the way to a new creation. It is especially with those whose idealizing and mirroring needs were not sufficiently met in childhood, that the analyst becomes the idealized one and the one who mirrors the analysand. The ascent or idealizing energies have to do with acquiring a spiritual center and a sense of meaning in our life. During the first stage of the analytic process the spirit archetype is stirred up in the idealized transference and this leads to an experience of a stabilizing center. At the same time a bridge to the inner world begins to form, a world that has been feared because of its shadow demons. If a child experiences being listened to, his or her ego is strengthened and a healthy relation to the unconscious can begin to develop. In therapy, as the adult "child" is heard, a newfound sense that life holds value and promise gains ground. Schwartz-Salant points out that in contrast to those who suffer from psychosis, these adults may find that:

. . . if the plunge into these feared emotional depths is taken, the belief that no rebirth can occur is often proven wrong. Rather than death or eternal chaos, one finds just the opposite: a true meeting with the Self, an inner reality that is dependable.[5]

This descent and the nascent experience of Self already imaged in the Advent wilderness must now be nourished, as the ascent and descent of psychic energies in the analytical relationship helps to solidify the emerging sense of self and of self-esteem.

There is a double aspect to our psyche, one facing upward to the sky and the sun, and the other facing downward to the darkness ruled by the moon. It is from the union of heaven and earth, sun and moon that psychic birth comes. In Christianity Mary is associated with the moon. As Mother her archetypal "roots" are found in the great Earth Mothers, for the moon is the feminine principle that governs earth's fertility, and the fertility goddesses are *chthonic,* meaning "of the earth." The themes related to earth goddesses—fertility, birth, death, rebirth—are mirrored in the waxing and waning cycles of the moon. In ancient times the Earth Mother was the single source of all life. According to Hesiod, Gaia or Earth gave birth to Ouranos, a being equal to her.[6] It was believed that parthenogenetic goddesses created all out of themselves without the help of male insemination. All life came out of the Earth Mother, including the heavens, the mountains and the rivers. According to Marija Gimbutas, in later Christian times

> The Birth Giver and Earth Mother fused with the Virgin Mary. Thus it is not surprising that in Catholic countries the worship of the Virgin surpasses that of Jesus. She is still connected with life ... water and miraculously healing springs, with trees, blossoms and flowers,

with fruits and harvest. She is pure, strong and just. In folk sculpture of the Mother of God, she is huge, and powerful, holding a tiny Christ on her lap.[7]

The ancient matriarchal belief in the self-generating goddesses is reflected not only in Catholic countries, but it is imprinted within our own psyche. Psychic birth comes out of the feminine, the "inner" feminine who is at once virgin and Mother.

Mary is virgin. This idea of virginity comes from ancient times when people saw no connection between sexual intercourse and the bearing of children. Women were thought to conceive by a transpersonal power through a part of the body: the ear or the thigh. It was thought that animals, birds or serpents impregnated them, or that a woman became pregnant by eating a certain fruit, or by visits from an ancestral spirit, or by the moon. In these primitive cultures the whole emphasis was on the fecundity of earth and of endless vegetation due to the creative qualities of motherhood. It is difficult for us to imagine such a culture, in which the emphasis was on the feminine creativity and the numinosity of pregnancy. In a matriarchy the source of life resides in the power of the woman. As heir to the Moon Goddess and the priestess, as well as to the Earth Mother, Mary, whom Augustine called the earth, receives the Spirit and conceives the child assuring the birth of Christ and the possibility for spiritual fruitfulness and redemption. "She does not conceive by man but conceives God himself by God himself," writes Jung.[8] Psychologically Mary represents the feminine aspect of the unconscious which tends to be "split off" in those who have suffered physical or mental abuse in childhood, and who, as result, suffer from a numbing sensation in affect and body awareness. Constellation of the Virgin archetype opens the possibility for a "sacred marriage" within psyche and the true birth or freeing of the fiery instincts of joy and love.

During the fourth week of Advent we reach the turning point when the "sacred marriage" takes place and the alchemical *albedo* begins to blend into the *rubedo,* that is, when darkness and cold give way to light and warmth. We might say that the Word becoming flesh represents psychologically the unity of ego consciousness and the deeper realms of the unconscious. When this happens we experience a greater sense of our own integrity, a sense of vitality and wholeness. As our own negativity and inner "critics" are transformed we may still fear our unconscious as something not to be trusted as a source of wisdom greater than our ego. It is often difficult to accept "not knowing."

Mary as virgin symbolizes this acceptance:

> . . . the angel Gabriel was sent by God to a town in Galilee called Nazareth, to a virgin betrothed to a man named Joseph . . . the virgin's name was Mary. He went in and said, "Rejoice, so highly favored! The Lord is with you." She was deeply disturbed by these words and asked herself what this greeting could mean, but the angel said to her, "Mary, do not be afraid you have won God's favor. Listen! You are to conceive and bear a son, and you must name him Jesus. . . ." Mary said to the angel, "How can this come about, since I am a virgin?" (Luke 1:26ff).

In Christianity angels are said to be present at our birth and at our death. They are, as well, guardians during our lifetime. They have an affinity with our soul. The alchemists viewed the angel as a helpful spirit, present always. This spirit was called, "the one who stands by."[9] In a psychological sense angels announce that unconscious contents want to be recognized and "incarnated." In this context angels are messengers between heaven and earth, representing forms of energy inaccessible to our ego, superior energies from the "other" world. Gabriel, for example, tells Mary something that she does not know, that she is especially favored by God. As images of psychic energies, angels are said to announce momentous changes that have irreversible effects on the entire personality. Like the voice in a dream, the message of an angel carries an authority so in tune with the deep desire of our being that though we may fear it, we must respond to its promise as to our own intuited destiny. Jung once said that analysis should release an experience "that falls upon us from above, an experience that has substance and body such as those things which occurred to the ancients. If I were going to symbolize it I would choose the Annunciation."[10] To be addressed by an angel is to experience the numinous from above as spirit and from below as desire.

In many representations of the annunciation we see a look of fear on Mary's face as if at the "intrusion" of a supernatural being. In other paintings, for example, those by Fra Angelico, she seems calm and inviting, unafraid of the angel's presence. In the scene below portrayed by Simone Martini, Mary seems "deeply disturbed" at the angel's greeting. She withdraws as if in fear and awe in the presence of the numinous. To the angel's message, "You shall conceive and bear a son," Mary does not hesitate to question, "How can this come about since I am a virgin?"

The word *parthenos* means unmarried woman, one not "under the law," that is, wedded to a man legally. Layard uses the word in the sense of "virgin forest," a picture of untrammelled nature before it is invaded by the town planners. The virgin's love is unbounded and unconditional. "Psychic virginity," not related to biological virginity, refers

"The Annunciation" by Simone Martini (Uffizi Gallery, Florence). (Courtesy Alinari/Art Resource, NY.)

to healing energies of the Self that lead to change in the way we feel about ourselves. Integrating these energies can lead us to psychic birth or the recovery of our true self, to the healing of the wound caused by early abuse and to the experience of our life journey as a gift of grace. If in childhood our "inner circle" or space has been psychically or physically invaded, constellation of the virgin archetype can be imaged as a "healed" inner space in both men and women that is close to the instinctual, and that makes the "new creation" possible.

This creative force, which in many men and women was sacrificed in childhood, can now begin to be felt. The hidden gods of sexuality and aggression begin to be accepted, not only as drives, but as aspects of a new body consciousness recognized and experienced. These "gods" begin to live when we can say, and for many it is for the first time, "I am," and "I need." Both men and women who find themselves caught in compulsive "drivenness" suffer from the negative inner forces of envy that are never far from us, especially if we have experienced early in our lives emotional rejection. We then may begin to find in compulsive activity or "doing" a way to bolster self-esteem. Often people complain that they have difficulty saying "no" when demands are made on them, or that they experience guilt when they do manage to say "no." The virgin, because she loves, can both open herself to others in love and, out of reverence for her own self, say "no." Esther Harding writes:

> The virgin is not reserved for one man . . . She remains virgin, even while being goddess of love . . . In the same way the woman who is virgin, one-in-herself, does what she does not because of any desire to please, not to be liked, or to be approved, even by herself; not because of

any desire to gain power over another, to catch his interest or love, but because what she does is true.[11]

When we can feel the energy of the "virgin" within us we can more fully awaken to the possibilities inherent in our own nature. It is as if the "inner circle" once victimized and raped is "sealed." "Sealing of the circle," writes Layard, "brings salvation,"[12] and the possibility for reconnecting to our own truth. The angel Gabriel's message for Mary and for ourselves is not that we must "do" something, rather it is that we must listen to who we "are," and accept ourselves as highly favored by God.

Annunciation corresponds to the moment, which is actually many moments, when the struggle with our negative inner demons leads to surrender to positive creative energies and to a realization of the God who cannot be grasped. In his treatise on the Trinity Jung compares the ages of the Father, Son, and Spirit to three stages of psychic development in which transition to the third stage brings "something like a recognition of the unconscious, if not actual subordination to it."[13] Opening to the inspiration of the Spirit is linked to religious experience which often has an erotic quality since, archetypally, pure spirit is an integration of spirit and instinct. In the representation of the annunciation by Henry O. Tanner the angel appears as light against a background of deep red. Light replaces word as a means of communication. On closer look we see that the light as "angel" not only appears at the left but follows along the lower left and center of the picture. This might suggest that the numinous energies do not only come from above to confront us but rise from the earth, that is, from our own instinct, need, and desire.[14] Our awakened consciousness comes not only as light from without, but as an inner light, as realization embodied.

The Spirit that comes to us from above is also moving us from below. It is the earthy feminine aspect of Spirit represented in alchemy by Mercurius. It is linked to our urges and deep desire, to our inner fire:

> Receiving and becoming pregnant by the Spirit implies that something new can be born out of that which "haunts" or "spirits" or "ghosts" us . . . out of our deep desire "soul pregnancy" can bear fruit in the flesh of every day life.[15]

If our individuation pattern moves us toward psychic birth of the true self, these energies as desires long hidden begin to awaken and, as we shall see, these energies long protected by our tightened and constricted bodies, can begin to emerge. The gods of anger, rage, aggressivity, compulsive sexuality can begin to surrender to the light side of the healing underground "gods," and we can begin to open ourselves to the Source that makes the impossible possible.

In response to Mary's question, "How can this be?" the angel replies:

> The Holy Spirit will come upon you and the power of the Most High will cover you with its shadow. And so the child will be holy and will be called Son of God. Know this, too; your kinswoman Elizabeth has, in her old age, herself conceived a son, and she whom people called barren is now in her sixth month, for nothing is impossible to God.

> "I am the handmaid of the Lord," said Mary, "let what you have said be done to me." And the angel left her (Luke 1:35–38).

It is when the "virgin" receptive to the Unknown, begins to live within us that the impossible becomes real. The angel calls to the realm of the "impossible." From our ego perspective, for something to be possible, means that it is able to be within the limitations of space and time. The possible is related to what can occur according to nature or what we are accustomed to. But what happens apart from our consciousness comes only when we surrender to the Unknown. What we cannot achieve on our own can happen from the unconscious as an intervention from "beyond," which we experience as numinous.

In Jung's view what heals us is our connection to the numinous:

> The main interest of my work is not concerned with the treatment of neuroses but rather with the approach to the numinous ... The approach to the numinous is the real therapy and inasmuch as you attain to the numinous experiences you are released from the curse of pathology.[16]

Can we say that the numinosum is the energy which becomes an internal center for those who have felt "cut-off" or abandoned or "empty," and, in a sense, unborn into their own lives? This is what Jung means—whether the experience evoking this energy comes from a biblical or religious image or from a dream image, a vision, or a synchronistic happening. The pain we suffer as children and adults, the struggles with inner destructive energies as well as problems and disappointments in our relationships with others are the prerequisites for the incarnation of our true self "bonded" with the transcendent.

Through entering the mystery of annunciation we allow ourselves to listen to and to respond to that within us which wants to be incarnated. And when we do this, Christ is born "now." Jung writes:

"Annunciation" by Henry O. Tanner (1898). Mary's "impregnation" by light can represent her own coming into self-awareness as well as her God-awareness. (Courtesy Philadelphia Museum of Art, The W. P. Wilstach Collection.)

Although the birth of Christ is an event that occurred but once in history, it has always existed in eternity. For the layman in these matters, the identity of a nontemporal, eternal event with a unique historical occurrence is something that is extremely difficult to conceive. He must, however, accustom himself to the idea that "time" is a relative concept and needs to be complemented by that of the "simultaneous" existence . . . of all historical processes. What exists . . . as an eternal process appears

> in time as an aperiodic sequence, that is to say, it is
> repeated many times in an irregular pattern . . .
>
> When these things occur in modern variants, therefore,
> they should not be regarded merely as personal epi-
> sodes, moods, or chance idiosyncrasies in people, but as
> fragments of the pleromatic process itself which broken
> up into individual events, occurring in time, is an essen-
> tial component or aspect of the divine drama.[17]

Jung refers here to the eternal process in a world mirrored
by the sequence of events in space and time. For when we
are not attuned to this world of energies which from our
ego-consciousness seems as remote as the domain of the
angels, a Gabriel coming with a message of divine birth
affects us as, indeed, "impossible."

Just as the alchemical "child" must descend to earth to
achieve wholeness, so we need to recover a sensitivity and
groundedness in our own "earth," our body. Mirroring helps
to ground us. If another reflects us to ourselves, we come to
sense who we are. This interchange between mother and
baby, for example, lays the "ground" for development of the
ego-identity. For our ancestors mirrors seemed miraculous,
because they felt that what they perceived in the mirror
really existed in its own right. Mirrors were also called
"shadow holders." The mirror can reveal to us a side that
we are not aware of. In the Greek mysteries of Dionysus, a
mirror was held up to the initiate which showed not "his
face but his Dionysian soul showing that the mirror reflected not the ego but its archetypal roots."[18] Jung saw
conscious-unconscious mirror symmetry, in that consciousness mirrors the Self as it brings it into time and space; the
Self reflects the ego, for example, in our dreams which

reflect unknown aspects of ourselves. St. Paul echoes this insight when he writes that now we see in a mirror dimly but then seeing face-to-face, we shall understand fully as we have been understood (1 Corinthians 13:12).

Psychologically speaking, if our early mirroring is good enough, if our infant babblings are responded to, we begin to develop a sense of security in ourselves. The one who mirrors says in effect, "I see you and I accept and love who you are." Donald Winnicott writes of the mirroring function between mother and baby:

> What does the baby see when he or she looks at the mother's face? I am suggesting that, ordinarily, what the baby sees is himself or herself. In other words the mother is looking at the baby and *what she looks like is related to what she sees there.* All this is too easily taken for granted . . . I can make my point by going straight over to the case of the baby whose mother reflects her own mood, or worse still, the rigidity of her own defenses. In such a case what does the baby see?[19]

Over a long period of time babies who do not get back what they give out suffer from a weakened self-esteem and from a hidden or overt grandiosity causing, as we have noted, the emotional highs and lows. Not only is the ego weakened but the child does not develop a true connection to his or her inner world, a healthy introversion, nor to the outer world and relationships with others.

Our own "dis-ease" leads us to the deeper dimension of psyche reflected over again, as we have seen, in the Advent imagery. For centuries Mary has been referred to as "Mirror of Justice (*speculum justiatae*), the one who reflects the Sun of Justice, and gives birth to the Just One (Isaiah 45). In Christianity this Just One refers to Jesus. In alchemy and in

Gnostic texts the Just One refers to the divine "spark" within. Mary as Mirror represents the initiative from the unconscious to restore on an archetypal level our wounded self. A Gnostic text describes this restoration through Mary, "my Mother, the Spirit," for in Gnostic teaching the Spirit is feminine, and Mary as mirror is

> the image of the invisible, virginal, perfect spirit—She became the Mother of everything, for she existed before them all, the mother-father (matropater). . . .[20]

For those on the way to psychic birth mirroring helps to restore the link to the self and to the Self as *Imago-Dei*. Mirroring helps to restore the link between conscious and unconscious, body and soul. It is the virgin who brings to life, who holds, nourishes and restores.

During the analytical process when a centering movement within helps us to recover a sense of meaning in our life, the descent begins into body awareness and consciousness. This is not to say that the two movements do not occur simultaneously, for the ego must be strong enough to accept and integrate the shadow. When grief and rage have been expressed in the "wilderness" sojourn, the nascent Self experience further strengthens the ego-identity. Now the "animals" within turn into helping energies as we get in touch with repressed sexuality and instinctual desire hidden for years under behavior dominated by "oughts" and "shoulds." Embodying happens as defensive armoring begins to unfreeze and as constricted breathing patterns, often developed in early childhood, release, enabling our body to find its own natural rhythm. Both in men and women blocked emotion and creativity lie in the earthy realm of the feminine, and during our individuation journey we must return again and again to the wilderness "fire." For even when the unconscious is deprived of its energy in part, it still remains continually active as a fire burning with one energy that combines the spiritual, instinctual, religious and sexual. We return to this fiery place to take back what belongs to us as true and to give up the false, an exchange that takes the form of sacrifice.

In the following text read during the fourth week of Advent it is as if Jesus speaks these words as he enters the world:

> You who wanted no sacrifice or oblation,
> prepared a body for me. . . .
> . . . then I said,
> "God, here I am! I am coming to obey your will."
> (Hebrews 10:5–10)

In part this text refers to Yahweh's disdain for the offering of animals prescribed by Law when these sacrifices are made simply to fulfill outward observance. What is desired by Yahweh is a true relationship based on sincerity of heart. Psychologically, this true relationship begins as the ego discovers that it is mirrored by something greater than itself, the Self, and that this Self guides the ego. The "way" toward this realization *is* the sacrifice, for sacrifice, following "God's will" involves the gradual acceptance and love of self.

Emotionally abused and abandoned children have felt worthless and empty for a good part of their lives. And the inner "no" to one's real self and the unconscious protection of a grandiose and successful persona has led further to a sense of guilt whenever the true instincts and desires are followed. This guilt stems from the negative side of the Mother archetype which seeks to prevent the unfolding of life. The guilt for living one's own life may lead to a need to

Joy

"repair" this guilt by "giving" to others. This pattern is often referred to as the "healer syndrome." Thus it may happen that in place of true giving and sacrifice, a false or neurotic "sacrifice" stemming from self-hatred can lead to a kind of masochistic self-destructive activity. But as we are released gradually from the power of the inner negative forces, a capacity for self-reflection is internalized and with it the possibility of life lived more fully, more joyfully. We can then be released from our compulsive drivenness and "doing" that compromise our real self, and make it difficult for us to be truly "for" others.

Incarnation means that spirit comes into body. As we become more conscious of who we are we become more present in our body, and Christ becomes present now. We do not "have" a body, we "are" our body, our spirit and instincts expressing themselves in our body. As Albert Pesso writes:

> Our bodies are endlessly and immediately reacting to everything that we really feel. Our body is a source of truth. Our soul speaks to us through our body. And all those symptoms inside are the energy of what we can become . . . the seed of the unborn self.[21]

For Jung body and psyche are one. Our body is the holy vessel prepared for the incarnating self. But when the feminine is repressed in a culture, we not only rape our forests and rivers, we begin to live in addicted, anorexic, obese or otherwise abused bodies.[22] Our "primary" personality which is open to giving and taking, full of wonder at life and secure in its "yes" and "no" wants release from our "false" personality which is stifled, armored, resigned or otherwise out of touch with its pleasurable energies. But as aspects of our real self, attuned both to the spiritual and the instinctual, begin to emerge, we can begin to feel the joy and wonder that longs to be "born" within us.

The approaching "birth" of the feminine-instinctual body self connected to our dark emotions and our spontaneity stir up joy and an urgency and desire to "be" ourselves and to be true to others. The emergence of "light" as freedom is connected in the mystery of Advent and the mystery of individuation with the "child of joy." At this stage if we have felt cut-off or in some way at war with our better self, we may begin to feel more accepting of ourselves and of others. This is not to say that the negative voices, "Oh, you don't deserve this!" are laid to rest forever, but the positive Mother energies and the virgin bearing her child speak of the inevitability of the new birth.

This psychological stage is represented in the Advent texts in the final reading of the fourth week which pictures Mary, the pregnant virgin, travelling over the hills of Galilee to visit her cousin Elizabeth, an old woman, who is also pregnant. As they meet, Elizabeth exclaims that the child in her womb leaps for joy (Luke 1:39). Any profound inner experience leads outward. It is the social function of the Self that unites us on a deep level. In touch with our real self, we become joyful, for the descent into "birth" brings with it a consciousness of our godlikeness. The meeting with the "other" brings a heightened sense of this mutual bond and a heightened sense of our uniqueness. Having gone through the journey or initiation toward recovery of ourself, we meet God and others in a new way.

> Life gains a double reality: on the one hand it begins to reflect the importance of social life and relationships, while, on the other it is grounded in the "unseen" world into which initiation has been granted.[23]

From a Jungian perspective this "unseen" world refers to the collective unconscious, a "world" inhabited by archetypal energies, personified now as virgin and Mother. It is the awakening within us of the healing feminine that mends the split between body and spirit, and enables us to realize that what was before a burden unwillingly borne and blamed perhaps on our family is now recognized as our own personality. We realize that in our godlikeness and weakness, our woundedness and our giftedness, we cannot live from anything except who we are.[24] The child graces us with a love of our own fate, and a recognition of its meaning as gift both for ourselves and for others.

In summary we have seen that the biblical text of the fourth week images for us the psychic process of imminent birth. The way leads us through a balancing and centering process imaged through the ascent and descent motif exemplified in alchemy and in the analytical process. Initiations lead us to participate in the transcendent world while grounding us more fully in the "now." What often happens as we live the Advent initiatory pattern as our personal journey, is a felt sense of inner power, our own and yet "given." The grace of this givenness is held by Mary who is virgin, *vas,* earth and mirror. Gabriel's presence to her is imaged in annunciation as an outer vision mirroring an inner realization of the impossible becoming possible. Indeed, Advent is an appropriate season to reflect again on the words of Angelus Silesius: "What good does Gabriel's 'Ave, Mary' do/ Unless he give me that same greeting too?"[25] Annunciation symbolizes that moment when we are strong enough to receive the angel messenger as enlightenment, when we can receive the Spirit of Love who both descends and ascends. Thus psychic pregnancy corresponds to our capacity to relate to our inner world as well as to our ability to give life and love to others. The virgin is not false in her giving because she is at home in herself and is thus open to love. She is comfortable in the realm of being and "unknowing," and can trust the source from which the impossible becomes possible. It is in this realm that our excitement, joy and creativity find a home. For they "belong" to us. Finding this inner treasure is our gift and the miracle which the alchemists sought as the crown of their work. This treasure is the divine child and it is, at the same time, our embodied self.

Conclusion

With Christmas we approach the *rubedo* of the alchemists. The color of Christmas is red, the red of passion, love and fire. In a letter to a man suffering from many physical symptoms Jung wrote, "You are in the midst of an inner confrontation with yourself." Referring to the alchemical fire Jung goes on to say that the "quickening of fire" means a transformation of the destructive fiery spirit into a *spiritus vitae*.[1] He questions whether in his friend "something that wants to go upwards has not taken a false route downwards into the body." Jung was pointing out something well-known today in the field of body psychotherapy. Our fire wants to be let out in creative activity, not to be pushed down. Body psychotherapists[2] speak of fiery "red" energy and receptive "blue" or parasympathetic energies in the body. In a healthy organism these energies are in balance. "Red" energy kept down festers in the body and can lead to psychosomatic symptoms. The alchemists' *rubedo* referred to the Gold, the Sun, and the Immortal Elixir of Life. It refers, as well, to our own transformation of destructive "fire" into a *spiritus vitae*.

In ancient Greece the question posed when someone came for healing was, "What do you lack?" In the context of Advent we ask, "What wants to be born in us?" For many of

142

us it is the inner "fire," the instinctual emotional life long hidden that wants to be "born." People often dream of children hurt, maimed, imprisoned, locked up in cellars. An analysand of mine dreamed of a mysterious locked cabinet in his house. Once, as he tried to open the cabinet, he discovered under one door, another thick glass door protecting the contents. This analysand had come to therapy complaining about his "drivenness." He felt out of touch with his body, complaining of a sense of "deadness" in his chest as if it were "covered with a lead plate." From childhood this man had protected the "fire" of his anger and rage which, in itself, held the key to his freedom and creativity.

Sometimes an analysand who has gone through the chaos and the wilderness journey, struggling with the destructive demons, still has difficulty retrieving the inner hidden treasure:

> It is as if the treasure, the inner precious part of oneself has been defended against and locked up for so long that even oneself cannot get in.[3]

But the unconscious is ahead of us and in our dreams there are often indications of transformation of the "dead," and access to the treasure.

An analysand dreamed:

> I am in a graveyard, looking at a particular grave that has in some way to do with me. There are three stones placed on a mound that I am looking up at, and I am arguing with someone about a fourth stone. I want it to be a grey color, like the other, but he wants it to be a strange color, like a bright red. It is also not round like the others, but has a rectangular shape. Finally, the reddish one is put in, and looking up there, I see there are now four stones. The fourth is very strange, not only in

the color red but it has designs on it, and a quadrated intersection of lines.[4]

To the man in the dream the dreamer associated someone ambitious, oriented to success in the world, representing a shadow side needing integration. The fourth, as red stone connects the dreamer to his own instinctual, creative energies of the "transformed" dead. But he prefers another grey stone. Grey is safe, red is risky. If grey has colored our lives from childhood, it prevents development of potential success, through living out the red side of our personality.

Another image, an image of child, comes to mind in connection with this changing of grey energies that may have dominated our lives. This image is related to fire and to the serpent, as principle of life and renewal. It is the image of the child Orc from William Blake's, "The Book of Urizen." Orc in his mother's womb appeared first as a serpent coiled and hissing. Gradually, as if recapping the evolutionary process, the serpent is formed as an infant and is born "with fierce flames." This child has miraculous powers to awaken the dead:

> The dead heard the voice of the child
> and began to awaken from sleep.
> All things heard the voice of the child
> And began to awake to life.
> (Blake, "The Book of Urizen")[5]

Orc as child carries both destructive and regenerative powers. We might say that he represents a "child" energy within us who has power to awaken us from patterns that limit and "deaden" us. As such, Orc represents an image of a child who "saves." Whatever our own experience has been, we carry within us the child that we were as well as a capacity to respond to other images of the "savior" child, most especially of the divine child.

Among the many motifs of the divine child in mythology, the most dominant is that of savior. The child comes to save us. The child manifests God in some form and is always born in lowly and insignificant settings. The savior comes out of poverty as hope out of despair. Another mythological motif related to the child is abandonment and persecution. This is seen clearly in King Herod's action upon hearing the news that a new king had been born. This motif is found in numerous fairy tales. It shows that the collective, the established power, fears the new, as we, too, at times, fear new possibilities emerging within ourselves, shaking us out of our old ways. Finally, the divine child in mythology is born in some miraculous way, for example, through impregnation by the sun. In Greek mythology, Danae is impregnated by Zeus in the form of a shower of gold. Sometimes the birth comes from an unusual part of the body, a finger or ear, or from nature associated with maternal elements such as water or a rock. That is to say, this birth is not "natural."

Psychologically viewed, the birth of a "child," that is, the freeing in us of unborn potential, is a psychic event. Jung writes of the mythological expression of these events as "birth."

> The "miraculous birth" tries to depict the way in which this genesis is experienced. Since it is a psychic genesis, everything must happen non-empirically, that is, by means of Virgin Birth, or by miraculous conception or by birth from unnatural organs . . .[6]

It is this sense that Jung refers to virgin birth as a psychic truth, a reality beyond our powers to grasp, a paradox of mystery. From the standpoint of religious dogma, too, the incarnation must be reverenced in its paradox which, in Jung's view, does more justice to what we with our limited minds cannot understand than any attempt at "clarity" could do.

This birth must be embodied, that is, experienced emotionally. That is, the "red" energy locked up inside us needs to be experienced and expressed. There are many ways that this embodying takes place. Jung referred to analysands who "danced their unconscious figures" or who sang or acted them. Attentiveness to our body through breath work, voice and movement help in our own grounding. Some approaches to body psychotherapy[7] focus on releasing conflictual energies through the peristaltic process of the intestine (sounds). While, symbolically the labyrinthine "coil" of the intestine ("the entrails") has been honored as a seat of divination, a way to know the will of the "god," both ancient Chinese practice in acupuncture and more modern research note that we "digest" emotion and visceral armoring through the action of the peristalsis. The goal of such body therapy is to put us in touch with our own bodily self-regulating center, and more fully, with our true self. In our day the intensity of our longing to be in touch with our body reflects the extent of our split-off feeling and our separation from the feminine realm.

Jung often said that only what is truly oneself heals. And the therapeutic process today bears some resemblance to that in ancient Greece. At the beautiful shrines that still dot the countryside of Greece, we are reminded that the one who approached there for healing was told first to go to a god-healer and to resort to the healing energies of the Earth Mother, and the body. During the course of the healing process the patient was to spend time sleeping in the sanctuary of the temple waiting for a healing dream. When the miracle of healing occurred, the patient, after making an offering to the god, was called *religiosus*. This term had nothing to do with church. It was to signify that the cure and the offering established a bond with the god, a bond that would last forever.

In the context of Advent we might say that the recovery of our "unborn" or unexperienced potential brings our healing and our at-one-ment with God. It is as if in hearing and answering the inner voice of the Baptist, the angel, the virgin, we come to hear our own voice and in so doing, to accept our fate. It is in accepting past rejection and abandonment as our "way" to salvation, that we begin to "see" the action of God. In looking back over our life we see that we were born into the family we needed, formed the relationships we needed, made the decisions we needed and that our path could not have been otherwise if we would discover the "gift" and meaning of our life, the "bond" with the god that comes with healing. For the god who wounds brings a gift to repay.

We have noted that in Jung's view Christ represents the possibility for reconnection with the archetype of wholeness because he is, par excellence, the whole or integral personality. The joy and merriment associated with his historical birth is always nuanced by the awareness of present and future suffering, rejection and abandonment. But this abandonment, or "death" in turn, is the prerequisite for birth or incarnation. It was through accepting the abandonment ("My God, My God, why hast thou forsaken me?" Matthew 27:47) that Christ won the treasure. Jung writes that though Christ felt deserted, it was

> because he had lived so fully and devotedly that he won through to the resurrection body ... We must all do just what Christ did. We must make our experiment. We

> must make mistakes. We must live our own vision of
> life. When we live like this we know Christ as a brother
> and God indeed becomes man, that is, God becomes
> man in ourselves.[8]

Christ's descent into the underworld, his wrestling with the
desert "demons" and his sense of abandonment by both
human and divine powers, led to resurrection or psychic
transformation. We see in the Advent mystery a similar initiatory pattern that, when experienced personally, can lead
to psychic birth.

As we have seen the child archetype is associated with
red, with energy, vitality, with earthy and bodily enjoyment.
Traditionally, Christmas as a celebration of the birth of
Christ has been the most human of feasts, with its music,
ritual, good food and drink and joyous partying. Combin-
ing the mystical and human dimensions as two aspects of
the same reality, Christmas glories in common earthy things
"charged" with the Infinite. Thus the birth of the child represents vitalizing energy and love as related to the human
and the divine, a relation expressed beautifully by Meister
Eckhart and St. Francis of Assisi.

It is the mystical dimension of the birth that captivates
Meister Eckhart:

> The supreme purpose of God is birth. He will not be
> content until his Son is born in us. Neither will the soul
> be content until the Son is born in it.[9]

For Eckhart, this eternal birth is always beginning anew as
God comes within our inner "stable." Psychologically this
means that libido that had been invested in outer objects,
making them seem all-powerful, returns to the soul. According to Eckhart the soul can begin to experience its own

truth. "Whatever leads you closest to this inner truth, you are to follow in all you do."[10]

For St. Francis, the historical birth of Christ was central, the child born in a manger surrounded by ox and ass. Appearing in the most unlikely of places, Christ shows himself first to lowly shepherds, and to the beasts of the field. Psychologically this means that new life comes from the least expected source, from the "devalued" animal side of the personality. Animals represent instinct which is the basis of human nature, for our humanness depends on how we express warmth and vitality. If our "animal" is imprisoned or neglected, it becomes destructive. Often in fairy tales healing comes after the hero has established a relationship with an insignificant or dangerous animal who, in turn, rewards him with blessing and good fortune.

The image of the Christmas crèche popularized by St. Francis, recalls a profound psychological truth that the divine child, as vital energy, appears in and connects us to the wounded and neglected side of our personality. The background for many crèche scenes is the mountain or cave. This image recalls the alchemical idea that the fetus is nourished and grows within the mountain as "oven" or incubator. The mountain represents the Center of the World, the place of new creation. In the crèche scene angels are pictured singing joyful tidings, announcing the birth of the Christ Child first to the shepherds who, psychologically, represent our earthy side, our sensation and instinct, while the kings, usually represented as approaching slowly from afar, represent spiritual and intellectual wisdom. It is, as the alchemists say, as if the new birth comes out of the earth and manifests itself within our own spontaneity and "earthiness." It takes "intellect" a longer time to approach the child. Finally, the star shines brightly above the crèche enfolding the scene in light after showing the "way." In the

Near East the star is said to enter the cave which becomes illuminated as a beacon to the wise men. Psychologically the star symbolizes hope fulfilled and a recognition that all through our lives we have been guided toward the fulfillment of our destiny.

In summary we can say that the healing pattern expressed in the Advent biblical imagery is not only a pattern of the tidings of salvation as seen from "without." The mystery of Advent leading us into a more personal or psychic birth is etched in our souls and on our bodies. The dogma of incarnation is rooted in our psyche and we do justice to it, not by minimizing the importance of the historical birth of Jesus Christ, but by taking to ourselves, as he did, the mystery of embodying the "divine nature" which we, too, are called to share (2 Peter 1:4). During the ancient winter solstice festivals the people knew that the sun which had "disappeared" would not return unless they helped it return. Through reenacting the "death" of the sun (king) and the chaos which ensured as a return to the *prima materia* from which a new beginning could come, they ritualized the myth of eternal return. This myth offers hope that the repressed "dead" are transformable and that out of chaos and darkness light returns.

As a metaphor for psychic birth of the true self Advent becomes a journey into separation, loss and pain . . . and into hope, release and joy. Experienced consciously as this journey, the Advent mystery can lead us through the winter darkness to the recovery of the hidden light as "child," as that "unborn" or imprisoned side of the personality, its instinctive needs, its warmth and spontaneity, and love. When this happens, Christmas becomes a celebration of Christ's birth, and of our own as well.

Selected Advent Texts

First Sunday of Advent

The vision of Isaiah son of Amoz, concerning Judah
and Jerusalem.
In the days to come
the mountain of the Temple of the Lord
shall tower above the mountains
and be lifted higher than the hills.
All the nations will stream to it,
peoples without number will come to it; and they
will say:

"Come, let us go up to the mountain of the Lord,
to the Temple of the God of Jacob
that he may teach us his ways
so that we may walk in his paths;
since the Law will go out from Zion,
and the oracle of the Lord from Jerusalem."
He will wield authority over the nations
and adjudicate between many peoples;

these will hammer their swords into ploughshares,
their spears into sickles.
Nation will not lift sword against nation,
there will be no more training for war.

O House of Jacob, come,
let us walk in the light of the Lord. (Isaiah 2:1–5)

Jesus said to his disciples:
"Be on your guard, stay awake, because you never know
when the time will come. It is like a man travelling abroad:
he has gone from home, and left his servants in charge, each
with his own task; and he has told the doorkeeper to stay
awake. So stay awake, because you do not know when the
master of the house is coming, evening, midnight, cock-
crow, dawn; if he comes unexpectedly, he must not find you
asleep. And what I say to you I say to all: Stay awake!"
(Mark 13:33–37)

You know "the time" has come: you must wake up now: our
salvation is even nearer than it was when we were con-
verted. The night is almost over, it will be daylight soon—let
us give up all the things we prefer to do under cover of the
dark; let us arm ourselves and appear in the light. Let us live
decently as people do in the daytime: no drunken orgies, no
promiscuity or licentiousness, and no wrangling or jealousy.
Let your armour be the Lord Jesus Christ; forget about satis-
fying your bodies with all their cravings. (Romans 13:11–14)

Jesus said to his disciples:

"As it was in Noah's day, so will it be when the Son of Man comes. For in those days before the Flood people were eating, drinking, taking wives, taking husbands, right up to the day Noah went into the ark, and they suspected nothing till the Flood came and swept all away. It will be like this when the Son of Man comes. Then of two men in the fields one is taken, one left; of two women at the millstone grinding, one is taken, one left.

"So stay awake, because you do not know the day when your master is coming. You may be quite sure of this that if the householder had known at what time of the night the burglar would come, he would have stayed awake and would not have allowed anyone to break through the wall of his house. Therefore, you too must stand ready because the Son of Man is coming at an hour you do not expect." (Matthew 24:37–44)

Jesus said to his disciples:

"There will be signs in the sun and moon and stars; on earth nations in agony, bewildered by the clamour of the ocean and its waves; men dying of fear as they await what menaces the world, for the powers of heaven will be shaken. And then they will see the Son of Man coming in a cloud with power and great glory. When these things begin to take place, stand erect, hold your heads high, because your liberation is near at hand. (Luke 21:25–28)

Second Sunday of Advent

The beginning of the Good News about Jesus Christ, the Son of God. It is written in the book of the prophet Isaiah:

"Look, I am going to send my messenger before you;
he will prepare your way.
A voice cries in the wilderness:
Prepare a way for the Lord,
     make his paths straight,"
and so it was that John the Baptist appeared in the wilderness, proclaiming a baptism for the forgiveness of sins. All
Judaea and all the people of Jerusalem made their way to
him, and as they were baptized by him in the river Jordan
they confessed their sins. John wore a garment of camel-
skin, and he lived on locusts and wild honey. In the course
of his preaching he said, "Someone is following me, someone who is more powerful than I am, and I am not fit to
kneel down and undo the strap of his sandals. I have baptized you with water, but he will baptize you with the Holy
Spirit." (Mark 1:1–8)

In the fifteenth year of Tiberius Caesar's reign when
Pontius Pilate was governor of Judaea, Herod tetrarch of
Galilee, his brother Philip tetrarch of the lands of Ituraea
and Trachonitis, Lysanias tetrarch of Abilene, during the
pontificate of Annas and Caiaphas, the word of God came
to John son of Zechariah, in the wilderness. He went through
the whole Jordan district proclaiming a baptism of repent-
ance for the forgiveness of sins, as it is written in the book of
the sayings of the prophet Isaiah:
"A voice cries in the wilderness:
Prepare a way for the Lord,
     make his paths straight.
Every valley will be filled in, every mountain and
     hill be laid low,
winding ways will be straightened

and rough roads made smooth.
And all mankind shall see the salvation of God."
(Luke 3:1–6)

Third Sunday of Advent

A man came, sent by God.
His name was John.
He came as a witness,
as a witness to speak for the light,
so that everyone might believe through him.
He was not the light,
only a witness to speak for the light.

This is how John appeared as a witness. When the Jews sent priests and Levites from Jerusalem to ask him, "Who are you?" he not only declared, but he declared quite openly, "I am not the Christ." "Well then," they asked, "are you Elijah?" "I am not," he said. "Are you the Prophet?" He answered, "No." So they said to him, "Who are you? We must take back an answer to those who sent us. What have you to say about yourself?" So John said, "I am, as Isaiah prophesied: a voice that cries in the wilderness: Make a straight way for the Lord."

Now these men had been sent by the Pharisees, and they put this further question to him, "Why are baptizing if you are not the Christ, and not Elijah, and not the Prophet?" John replied, "I baptize with water; but there stands among you—unknown to you—the one who is coming after me; and I am not fit to undo his sandal-strap." This happened at Bethany, on the far side of the Jordan, where John was baptizing. (John 1:6–8, 19–28)

Be patient, brothers, until the Lord's coming. Think of a farmer: how patiently he waits for the precious fruit of the ground until it has had the autumn rains and the spring rains! You too have to be patient; do not lose heart, because the Lord's coming will be soon. Do not make complaints against one another, brothers, so as not to be brought to judgment yourselves; the Judge is already to be seen waiting at the gates. For your example, brothers, in submitting with patience, take the prophets who spoke in the name of the Lord. (James 5:7-10)

Fourth Sunday of Advent

In the sixth month the angel Gabriel was sent by God to a town in Galilee called Nazareth, to a virgin betrothed to a man named Joseph, of the House of David; and the virgin's name was Mary. He went in and said to her, "Rejoice, so highly favored! The Lord is with you." She was deeply disturbed by these words and asked herself what this greeting could mean, but the angel said to her, "Mary, do not be afraid; you have won God's favor. Listen! You are to conceive and bear a son, and you must name him Jesus. He will be great and will be called Son of the Most High. The Lord God will give him the throne of his ancestor David; he will rule over the House of Jacob for ever and his reign will have no end." Mary said to the angel, "But how can this come about, since I am a virgin?" "The Holy Spirit will come upon you" the angel answered "and the power of the Most High will cover you with its shadow. And so the child will be holy and will be called Son of God. Know this too: your kinswoman Elizabeth has, in her old age, herself conceived a son, and she whom people called barren is now in her sixth month, *for nothing is impossible to God*. "I am the hand-maid of the Lord," said Mary "let what you have said be done to me." And the angel left her. (Luke 1:26–38)

This is what Christ said, on coming into the world: "You who wanted no sacrifice or oblation, prepared a body for me. You took no pleasure in holocausts or sacrifices for sin; then I said, just as I was commanded in the scroll of the book, 'God, here I am! I am coming to obey your will.'" Notice that he says first: You did not want what the Law lays down as the things to be offered, that is: the sacrifices, the oblations, the holocausts and the sacrifices for sin, and you took no pleasure in them; and then he says: Here I am! I am coming to obey your will. He is abolishing the first sort to replace it with the second. And this will was for us to be made holy by the offering of his body once and for all by Jesus Christ. (Hebrews 10:5–10)

Mary set out at that time and went as quickly as she could to a town in the hill country of Judah. She went into Zecha-riah's house and greeted Elizabeth. Now as soon as Eliza-beth heard Mary's greeting, the child leapt in her womb and Elizabeth was filled with the Holy Spirit. She gave a loud cry and said, "Of all women you are the most blessed, and blessed is the fruit of your womb. Why should I be hon-oured with a visit from the mother of my Lord? For the moment your greeting reached my ears, the child in my womb leapt for joy. Yes, blessed is she who believed that the promise made her by the Lord would be fulfilled." (Luke 1:39–45)

Notes

Introduction

1. Raymond Blakney, trans., *Meister Eckhart: A Modern Translation* (New York: Harper and Row, 1941), p. 95.

2. C.G. Jung, *Psychology and Alchemy,* (translated by R.F.C. Hull. Bollingen Series XX. Volume 12, Collected Works, Princeton: Princeton University Press, 1963) p. 185.

3. *Ibid,* p. 14.

4. C.G. Jung, *Letters* (Princeton: Princeton University Press, 1973, Volume 1), p. 65.

5. See Christopher Lasch, *The Culture of Narcissism* (New York: W.W. Norton & Co., Inc., 1979).

6. Stephen Kurtz, C.S.W., *The Art of Unknowing* (Northvale: Jason Aronson, Inc., 1983), p. 170.

7. *Ibid.*

8. T.S. Eliot, *The Waste Land, Complete Poems and Plays* (New York: Harcourt, Brace and World, Inc., 1971), p. 49.

9. C.G. Jung, *op. cit.* p. 282.

10. J.C. Cooper, *An Illustrated Encyclopedia of Traditional Symbols* (London: Thames & Hudson, 1978), p. 90.

1. Anticipation

1. Adrian Nocent, *The Liturgical Year* (Collegeville: The Liturgical Press, 1965) Volume 1, p. 263.

2. Harvey Cox, *Feast of Fools: A Theological Essay on Festival and Fantasy* (Cambridge: Harvard University Press, 1969), p. 30.

3. *Ibid.*

4. Theodor Gaster, *New Year: Its History, Customs and Superstitions* (New York: Abelard Schuman, 1955), p. 2.

5. *Ibid.,* p. 3.

6. *Ibid.,* p. 6.

7. C.G. Jung, *Memories, Dreams, and Reflections,* ed. Aniela Jaffe (New York: Pantheon Books, 1961), p. 194.

8. *Ibid.*

9. Mircea Eliade, *The Myth of Eternal Return* (Princeton: Princeton University Press, 1954), p. 5.

10. *Ibid.,* p. 6.

11. Clement, Miles. *Christmas in Ritual and Tradition* (London: T. Fisher Unwin, 1912), p. 166.

12. Gaster, *op. cit.,* p. 52.

13. *Ibid.,* p. 53.

14. Eliade, *op. cit.,* p. 68.

15. Miles, *op. cit.,* p. 167.

16. *Ibid.*

17. Mircea Eliade, *Myths, Dreams, and Mysteries* (New York: Harper and Row, 1960), p. 53.

18. Jung, *Memories, Dreams, and Reflections,* pp. 101–102.

19. Donald W. Winnicott, *Holding and Interpretation* (New York: Grove Press, 1972), p. 32.

20. Eliade, *The Myth of Eternal Return,* p. 82.

21. Anne Sexton, *The Awful Rowing Toward God* (Boston: Houghton Mifflin, 1975), p. 61.

22. Marija Gimbutas, *Language of the Goddess: Unearthing the Hidden Symbols of Western Civilization* (New York: Harper and Row, 1989), p. 100.

2. Longing

1. Eliade, *Myths, Dreams, and Mysteries,* p. 157.

2. *Ibid.,* p. 158.

3. *Ibid.,* p. 160.

4. Vera van der Heydt, "Alchemy," Guild of Pastoral Psychology Lecture no. 105. (September 1959), p. 6.

5. Mircea Eliade, "The Myth of Alchemy," *Parabola* (August, 1978), p. 11.

6. C.G. Jung, *Mysterium Coniunctionis,* (translated by R.F.C. Hull. Bollingen Series XX. Volume 14, Collected Works, Princeton: Princeton University Press, 1963), p. 127.

7. C.G. Jung, *Man and His Symbols* (New York: Dell Publishing Co.), p. 85.

8. C.G. Jung, *Seminar on Alchemy,* p. 85. (This text consists of notes on lectures given by Jung at the University of Zurich from November 1940 to July 1941. They have not been "officially" published though most of the material can be found in Jung's *Psychology and Alchemy.* The seminar notes printed by Karl Schippert & Co. Zurich can be found in most C.G. Jung Institute libraries.)

9. *Ibid.,* p. 45.

10. *Ibid.,* p. 121.

11. Jung, *Mysterium Coniunctionis,* p. 229.

12. Marie-Louise von Franz, *Alchemy: An Introduction to the Symbolism and the Psychology* (Toronto: Inner City Books, 1980), p. 168.

13. Edward Edinger, *Anatomy of the Psyche: Alchemical Symbolism in Psychotherapy* (La Salle: Open Court Publishers, 1985), p. 83.

14. Ann Belford Ulanov, *Picturing God* (Boston: Cowley Publications, 1986), p. 187.

15. *Ibid.*

3. Hope

1. Heinz Kohut, *How Does Analysis Cure?* (Chicago: University of Chicago Press, 1984), p. 131.

2. Karl Menninger, "Hope," *The American Journal of Psychiatry* (1959) 483.

3. Walter Zimmerli, *Man and His Hope in the Old Testament* (London: SCM Press, 1971), p. 8.

4. Henri Desroche, *The Sociology of Hope* (London: Routledge & Kegan Paul, 1979), p. 1.

5. *Ibid.,* p. 3.

6. Adrian Nocent, O.S.B., *The Liturgical Year,* p. 27.

7. J.C. Cooper, *An Illustrated Encyclopedia of Traditional Symbols,* p. 58.

8. Robert E. Hobson, *Forms of Feeling: The Heart of Psychotherapy* (New York: Tavistock Publications), pp. 268–270.

9. C.G. Jung, *Memories, Dreams, and Reflections,* p. 194.

10. *Ibid.*

11. C.G. Jung and E. Kerenyi, *Essays on a Science of Mythology* (New York: Pantheon Books, 1959), p. 79.

12. *Ibid.,* p. 39.

13. *Ibid.,* p. 40.

14. C.G. Jung, *Symbols of Transformation* (translated by R.F.C. Hull. Bollingen Series XX. Volume 5 Collected Works, Princeton: Princeton University Press, 1956), p. 82.

15. C.G. Jung, *Psychology and Religion: West and East* (translated by R.F.C. Hull. Bollingen Series XX. Volume 11 Collected Works, Princton: Princeton University Press, 1958), p. 441.

16. C.G. Jung, *Psychology and Alchemy,* p. 10.

17. C.G. Jung, *Two Essays on Analytical Psychology* (translated by R.F.C. Hull. Bollingen Series XX. Volume 7 Collected Works, Princeton: Princeton University Press, 1966), p. 177.

18. C.G. Jung, *Seminar on Alchemy,* p. 214.

19. Cooper, *op. cit.,* p. 70.

20. Marie-Louise von Franz, ed. *Aurora Consurgens* (London: Routledge & Kegan Paul, 1966), p. 203.

4. Fear

1. Erich Neumann, *The Great Mother: An Analysis of the Archetype* (Princeton: Princeton University Press, 1955), pp. 45–46.

2. Mario Jacoby, *Longing for Paradise* (Boston: Sigo Press, 1985), p. 9.

3. Ann and Barry Ulanov, *Religion and the Unconscious* (Philadelphia: Westminster Press, 1975), p. 163.

4. Jung, *Psychology and Alchemy,* p. 74.

5. Edinger, *Anatomy of the Psyche,* p. 11.

6. E. Dickinson, *Poems of Emily Dickinson* (New York: Avenel Books, 1982), p. 196.

7. Elaine Pagels, *The Gnostic Gospels* (New York: Vintage Books, 1981), p. 172.

5. Anger

1. T.S. Eliot, *The Cocktail Party, T.S. Eliot: The Complete Poems and Plays* (New York: Harcourt, Brace & World, 1973), pp. 364–5.

2. C.G. Jung, *The Development of Personality* (translated by R.F.C. Hull. Bollingen Series XX. Volume 17, Collected Works, Princeton: Princeton University Press, 1954), p. 176.

3. Paul Diel, *Symbolism in the Bible: Its Psychological Significance* (San Francisco: Harper & Row, 1986), p. 154.

4. Alice Miller, *The Drama of the Gifted Child and the Search for the True Self* (London: Faber and Faber, 1979), p. 28.

5. Walter Wink, *John the Baptist in the Gospel Tradition* (London: Cambridge University Press, 1968), p. 20.

6. Nathan Schwartz-Salant, *Narcissism and Character Transformation: The Psychology of the Narcissistic Character Disorder* (Toronto: Inner City Books, 1982), p. 179.

7. Miller, *op. cit.,* p. 28.

8. Quoted in Schwartz, *op. cit.,* p. 24.

9. *Ibid.,* pp. 76–83.

10. Mircea Eliade, *Rites and Symbols of Initiation* (New York: Harper Torchbooks, 1958), p. 135.

11. Anthony Stevens, *Archetype: A Natural History of the Self* (London: Routledge & Kegan Paul, 1982), p. 114.

12. von Franz, *Aurora Consurgens,* p. 336.

6. Joy

1. Jung, *Psychology and Religion: West and East,* p. 54.

2. C.G. Jung, *The Practice of Psychotherapy* (translated by R.F.C. Hull. Bollingen Series XX. Volume 16, Princeton: Princeton University Press, 1966), p. 273.

3. Jung, *Mysterium Coniunctionis,* p. 218.

4. *Ibid.,* p. 219.

5. Schwartz-Salant, *op. cit.,* p. 66.

6. Mircea Eliade, *Myths, Rites, Symbols: A Mircea Eliade Reader,* eds. Wendell C. Beane and William G. Doty (New York: Harper & Row, 1975), p. 204.

7. Gimbutas, *op. cit.,* p. 319.

8. C.G. Jung, *Letters,* ed., Gerhard Adler, Volume 1, (Princeton: Princeton University Press, 1973), p. 466.

9. Jung, *Seminar on Alchemy,* p. 154.

10. von Franz, *Alchemy: An Introduction to the Symbolism and the Psychology,* p. 269.

11. Esther Harding, *Women's Mysteries* (New York: Bantam Books, 1971), p. 145.

12. John Layard, *The Virgin Archetype* (Zurich: Spring Publications, 1972), p. 297.

13. Jung, *Psychology and Religion: West and East,* p. 285.

14. I am indebted to Dr. Paul Brutsche for this observation.

15. David Miller, "Womb of God, Body of the Sun: Reflections on Christian Imagery of the Virgin and the Moon" in *Images of the Untouched,* eds. J. Stroud and G. Thomas (Dallas: Spring Publications, 1982), p. 93.

16. Jung, *Letters,* p. 377.

17. Jung, *Psychology and Religion: West and East,* pp. 400–401.

18. Schwartz-Salant, *op. cit.,* p. 90.

19. Quoted in Donald Kalched, "Narcissism and the Search for Interiority," *Quadrant,* Volume 13 (1980), no. 2, p. 68.

20. Pagels, *op. cit.,* p. 62.

21. Deldon McNeely, *Touching: Body Therapy and Depth Psychology* (Toronto: Inner City Books, 1987), p. 55.

22. See studies by Marion Woodman: *The Owl Was a Baker's Daughter, Addiction to Perfection, the Pregnant Virgin,* all published by Inner City Books, Toronto.

23. Schwartz-Salant, *op. cit.,* p. 169.

24. Jung, *Mysterium Coniunctionis,* p. 231.

25. *Ibid.,* p. 319.

Conclusion

1. Jung, *Letters,* p. 403.

2. Gerda Boyesen, "The Dynamics of Psychosomatics," *Journal of Biodynamic Psychology* (Winter 1982) no. 3, pp. 55–69. Biodynamic Body Psychotherapists speak of "red" and "blue" energies in the body. Through balancing these energies we try to free the emotional cycle which in many people has become restricted due to inhibited breathing. See also David Boadella. *Lifestreams* New York: Routledge & Kegan Paul, 1987.

3. Schwartz-Salant, *op. cit.,* p. 169.

4. *Ibid.,* p. 130.

5. William Blake, "The Book of Urizen," *Blake's Poetry and Designs,* ed. by Mary Lynn Johnson and John E. Grant (New York: W.W. Norton & Co., 1979), p. 155.

6. C.G. Jung, *The Archetypes and the Collective Unconscious* Volume 9(1) Collected Works (Princeton: Princeton University Press, 1963), p. 166.

7. Boyesen, *op. cit.,* p. 70.

8. Kalched, *op. cit.,* p. 74.

9. Raymond Blakney, trans., *Meister Eckhart: A Modern Translation,* p. 8.

10. *Ibid.*